GOLD DEALING: YOUR PATH TO SUCCESS WITH OR WITHOUT CAPITAL

INTRODUCTION

Becoming a gold dealer today offers a fantastic opportunity to earn a reliable and safe income while providing a valuable service to the public, helping them manage their bills and financial needs. Beyond that, you'll also play a crucial role in gold recycling, which contributes to environmental sustainability by reducing the need for new mining and conserving precious resources. By participating in this industry, you support eco-friendly practices and promote a greener future. It's a win-win-win no brainer!

There are few barriers to entry in this area and currently there are no regulations that directly control the business, though there are many regulations that you will need to adhere to (see Chapter 6)

Whilst this book was initially aimed at the UK market only, the information contained therein applies around the world, though local and national laws may vary. Check these in your own country, but regardless of whether you live in the USA the EU or the UK, this book will help you start a lucrative

This book has been written to give you all the information tips and tricks you need to become a full-time gold buyer, with or without capital. That is right! Further into this book you will realize that capital whilst important, is no barrier to entry here. Enjoy!

ABOUT ME.

I have worked in the gold business, with my partner for over 40 years and continue to run one of the UK's largest gold buying businesses. In this book I will be explaining how to make money as a gold trader/dealer. This book contains information, tips, and tricks to help you make a substantial income in this very much in demand industry. But no amount of expertise will help you unless you have the right approach and attitude to gold and precious metal buying so let's start with you.

ABOUT YOU.

You have to ask yourself if you are right for this business. All the **best** gold dealers I know have several traits in common as follows.

1/ They put the Customer First.

2/ They are Honest

3/ They are scrupulously careful and meticulous

4/ They do what they say, i.e. pay what they say they pay.

5/ They don't gamble on gold and silver purities etc.

6/ They understand the metals and the math!

7/ They are never greedy

If this checklist describes the sort of person, you are/could be then you will be well suited to the business. As you will see in following chapters these 7 points help you find a gold buyer that you can do business with

Becoming a gold dealer is not a get rich quick scheme and neither is it just for rich people, those with money to spare. Though it is a common belief that you cannot be a gold buyer/ dealer without tons of capital,

My partner and I achieved our success in the gold business, starting out with just £50 in the 1990's and the same path can be trodden today You do NOT need vast sums to set up in this business, but you do have to follow a clear path, one I have laid out carefully for you here in the following chapters.

For this chapter, however we have to begin at the beginning and the very first step in all of this is to familiarize yourself with the different type of precious metals and their carats and purities. Don't skip this section as you will need full knowledge in order to successfully buy and sell gold and other precious metals here in the UK, the EU, and the USA

NB this book assumes you know nothing. If you know your gold, then why not speed read the next couple of chapters and check your knowledge but if this is all new to you then the following chapters will be invaluable.

CHAPTER 1. SCRAP & NON-SCRAP GOLD & SILVER

Before we get into all the carats and quality /purity of gold and silver etc. it is worth mentioning right at the outset the difference between what is scrap gold/silver and what is not.

Scrap gold is any gold that as a piece of jewellery is either not in demand or has some form of damage requiring costly refurbishment e.g. wear, deep scratches, damage to the gemstone and/or hallmark; out of fashion; too small or too large to be economically viable for sale etc.

When it comes to selling gold, it's essential to distinguish between scrap gold and items that may have higher value as jewellery. Understanding the difference can help you maximize your returns and make informed decisions. It can also prevent a nasty situation where you inadvertently value an item as scrap when it is not, potentially upsetting a customer who is trying to sell gold to you. Many people treasure certain pieces of jewellery e.g. heirlooms etc so your appraisal must be spot on

What is Scrap Gold?

Scrap gold refers to any gold item that is sold primarily for the value of its metal content rather than its design or condition. This category includes:

- Broken or Damaged Jewellery: Pieces that are heavily worn, broken, or irreparably damaged.

- Outdated or Unfashionable Items: Jewellery that is no longer in style or has limited market appeal.

- Non-Hallmarked Items: Items without proper hallmarks, making their gold content uncertain.

- Small Fragments: Parts of jewellery, like clasps or links, which have little aesthetic or functional value.

These items are typically melted down and refined to extract the pure gold, which is why they are valued solely based on their gold content.

NB Colours. Scrap gold can be white, yellow or rose gold. There is no difference in value nor worth between them. White gold means that the item is rhodium plated, while rose gold means the item has more copper than silver in its mix.

What is Not Scrap Gold?

Not all gold items should be considered scrap. Certain pieces can be worth more than their metal content due to various factors:

- Fine Jewellery and Watches: High-end pieces from renowned brands like Cartier, Rolex, Tiffany, and Bulgari often retain significant value beyond their gold content.

- Antique and Vintage Jewellery: Items with historical significance or those that are rare and collectible.

- Designer Jewellery: Pieces from well-known designers that are in good condition and maintain their aesthetic and market value.

- Jewellery with Valuable Gemstones: Rings, necklaces, and other items that feature large or high-quality diamonds, sapphires, rubies, or emeralds.

Factors Affecting Value Beyond Scrap

1. Condition: The state of the jewellery significantly impacts its value. Items that are scratched, chipped, or have worn-down hallmarks might only be worth their gold content. Conversely, well-maintained pieces can fetch higher prices.

2. Hallmarks: Proper hallmarks verify the purity of gold. UK hallmarks are particularly trusted, while foreign hallmarks can sometimes be less reliable. Items with clear, reputable hallmarks are often more valuable.

3. Market Demand: Trends in fashion and buyer preferences affect jewellery value. Even high-quality items might be considered scrap if they are out of style or not in demand. However, antique and vintage pieces from recognized brands typically maintain higher value.

4. Refurbishing Costs: The potential cost of refurbishing a piece can lower its resale value. Scratches, stone wear, or other damage might necessitate repairs, which impacts the final price a buyer is willing to pay.

Conclusion

Deciding whether gold jewellery is worth more than scrap requires a careful assessment of its condition, hallmark, market demand, and potential refurbishing costs. Items from prestigious brands or those featuring valuable gemstones are often worth more than their weight in gold.

As a gold buyer you are primarily interested in buying scrap items. If you start out in the very difficult field of fine gems and jewellery, then you will be likely walking straight into a minefield.

Make no mistake, the public value certain items of jewellery above others. If you believe an item to be scrap then point out the reasons why, but until you have sourced a buyer of upmarket gemstones etc it is best that you suggest to any customer to go the auction route for these items. Remember when we said at the beginning of this book that good gold buyers are never greedy? Don't make any offers on diamond/precious stone jewellery or named items unless you are able to sell on easily . If you really do want to get into selling fine jewellery and antique etc items then I have written a chapter at the end of this book i.e. chapter --- but for now, we are talking scrap and that will be your main business.

A word about Silver

If a silver item is out of fashion, or damaged, or worn/rubbed or the hallmarks damaged or missing, again it is scrap.

Chapter 1 Summary: Scrap and Non-Scrap Gold and Silver

In this chapter, we delved into the essential distinctions between scrap and non-scrap gold and silver, which is crucial for maximizing returns and making informed decisions in the gold dealing business.

Key Points:

1. Understanding Scrap Gold:

- **Definition:** Scrap gold is any gold item valued primarily for its metal content rather than design or condition.
- **Examples:**
  - Broken or damaged jewellery.
  - Outdated or unfashionable pieces.
  - Non-hallmarked items.
  - Small fragments or parts of jewellery.

2. Recognizing Non-Scrap Gold:

- **Higher Value Items:**
  - Fine jewellery and watches from renowned brands (e.g., Cartier, Rolex, Tiffany, Bulgari).
  - Antique and vintage jewellery with historical significance.
  - Designer jewellery in good condition.
  - Jewellery with large or high-quality gemstones (e.g., diamonds, sapphires, rubies, emeralds).

3. Factors Affecting Value Beyond Scrap:

- **Condition:** Well-maintained items fetch higher prices; damaged items may only be worth their gold content.

- **Hallmarks:** Proper hallmarks, especially UK hallmarks, verify gold purity and increase value.
- **Market Demand:** Fashion trends and buyer preferences impact value; high-quality but out-of-style items might still be considered scrap.
- **Refurbishing Costs:** Costs of repairing scratches, stone wear, or other damage can lower resale value.

4. Importance of Accurate Appraisal:

- **Customer Trust:** Avoid valuing heirlooms or treasured pieces as scrap to maintain customer trust.
- **Informing Customers:** Explain why an item is considered scrap and suggest auction routes for valuable non-scrap items.

5. Dealing with Silver:

- **Scrap Silver:** Items that are out of fashion, damaged, worn, or have damaged/missing hallmarks are considered scrap.

Conclusion:

Carefully assessing the condition, hallmark, market demand, and refurbishing costs of gold jewellery is essential to determine its value beyond scrap. As a gold buyer, focusing primarily on scrap items is advisable unless you have established buyers for fine jewellery and gemstones. Always approach the valuation process with integrity to maintain customer trust and avoid potential pitfalls in the market.

CHAPTER 2. GOLD SILVER, PLATINUM AND PALLADIUM WEIGHTS CARATS AND PURITIES

Weights

All gold and silver are measured in gram weight. Some still talk about troy ounces, as opposed to cooking ounces. You will need to understand all these measures and will need scales that measure in grams.

Gram: A gram is the most common unit of measurement for gold and silver in the jewellery and precious metals industry. One gram is equal to one-thousandth of a kilogram and is a standard metric unit.

Troy Ounce vs. Ounce (Avoirdupois Ounce): A troy ounce is a unit of measurement traditionally used in the precious metals industry. One troy ounce is equivalent to approximately 31.1035 grams. This differs from the avoirdupois ounce (commonly used in cooking and grocery measurements), which is equal to approximately 28.3495 grams. It's essential to use troy ounces when dealing with precious metals to ensure accuracy in weight and value calculations.

Understanding these weight measurements is crucial in the gold dealing business. Accurate scales calibrated to measure in grams and troy ounces will ensure you correctly assess the value of the gold and silver you buy and sell.

Carats |Purities

Precious metals come in many forms, bars, coins, jewellery, industrial scrap, and waste and so on. Gold, Silver, Platinum, and Palladium all vary in purities. With Gold, we talk about its purity in terms of carat.

Wiki defines a carat as "The karat (US spelling, symbol k or Kt) or carat (UK spelling, symbol c or Ct) is a fractional measure of purity for gold alloys in parts fine per 24 parts whole."

The origin of the "carat is as follows This system of indicating the relative proportion of gold originated with a medieval coin called a mark. A mark weighed 24 carats (in this case, the carat was the same as that used in the weighing of gems and was theoretically equal to the weight of the seed of the carob tree).

Actually, Gold can actually be any carat right up to 24 carat gold.

The most popular carats are of course.

9 carat (375/1000)

12 carat (500/1000

14 carat (750/1000)

15 carat gold 625/1000

18 carat (375/1000)

22 carat (375/1000)

24 carat (375/1000)

But You can also find 8 carat Gold in Germany (marked with 333); 10 carat Gold in mainly the USA ; 19 carat Gold from Portugal; 21carat Gold which is mainly Asian jewellery and anywhere in between i.e. I tested a piece of gold last week that was 17.6 carat gold. These odd results will be discussed later in this book but for now let's focus on the usual carats (UK and EU)

9 Carat Gold. 9c, 9k, 9ct, 375

9 carat gold is the most common form of gold sold in the UK. This alloy contains 37.5% pure gold, with the remaining 62.5% made up of other metals such as silver, copper, and zinc. These additional metals contribute to the durability and hardness of 9 carat gold, making it tougher and more hard-wearing compared to higher carat golds like 14, 18, and 22 carat gold. It can come in various shades, including yellow gold, white gold (achieved through rhodium plating), and rose gold, which has extra copper added to give it a distinctive pinkish hue. In the UK, most gold sold is 9 carat, and it is easily identified by the hallmark number "9" or "375," indicating its gold content of 375 parts per 1,000. The value of 9 carat gold remains consistent regardless of whether it is yellow, rose, or white. You can commonly find 9 carat gold in rings, bracelets, chains, pendants, bangles, and charms, with or without stones.

Most of the gold you will find on your travels will be 9 carat. if you are based in the UK will be 9 carat gold and 14 carat in Europe. 18 carat gold is also common in the UK as is 22carat gold and of course pure gold.

10 carat Gold 10c 10k 416

10 carat gold, often marked as "10K" or "417," contains 41.7% gold, with the remainder composed of other metals like silver, copper, and zinc. This alloy makes 10 carat gold more durable and resistant to scratching compared to higher purity gold, making it a popular choice in the United States for everyday jewelry that can withstand regular wear. The reduced gold content also makes 10 carat gold more affordable than higher carat options, offering consumers the beauty and prestige of gold at a lower price point. Despite its lower purity, 10 carat gold maintains a warm appearance, though not as richly colored as 14 or 18 carat gold, and is suitable for a wide range of jewelry, including rings, bracelets, and necklaces.

12 carat Gold 12ct, 12k, 0.500, 500

12-carat gold, which is comprised of 50% pure gold, has historical and modern uses in England, particularly in the jewellery sector. While not as common today due to preferences for higher carat values in luxury items, 12-carat gold was historically used more widely when robustness was desired alongside some level of affordability. Today, its use in England is more limited, often reserved for specific types of jewellery that benefit from the greater hardness provided by the additional alloys. This type of gold offers a cost-effective alternative for consumers seeking the aesthetic and intrinsic value of gold at a lower price point, making it suitable for everyday jewellery that withstands regular wear and tear better than its higher carat counterparts.

14 Carat Gold. 14k, 14c, 14ct 585

14 carat gold, which contains 58.5% pure gold, is a higher quality gold compared to 9 carat gold. It is often found in the UK and abroad, including countries like Turkey and throughout the European Union. Like other gold alloys, it can come in yellow, white (with rhodium plating), or rose (with added copper) varieties. It is identified by the hallmark number "14" or "585," representing 585 parts of gold per 1,000. While 14 carat gold is durable and more gold-rich than 9 carat gold, it is still tougher than 18 and 22 carat gold. A notable caution is necessary when dealing with foreign 14 carat gold hallmarks; some countries without stringent hallmarking laws may have inaccurately marked pieces, making scientific testing essential for verification, especially if the hallmark appears rough or ill-defined. Historically, old UK gold jewellery may also feature 15 carat gold, marked by "625."

14 carat gold is something to be wary of, as a gold buyer, especially as it is not a UK standard hallmark and in some countries on the continent hallmarks are done by the jewellery manufacturers the section on hallmarking below will give you more help with this. There is a world of difference between a rough hallmark that looks like it has been scratched in and one made.

15 Carat Gold 15c 15k 15ct 625

15-carat gold, consisting of 62.5% pure gold mixed with other metals such as silver and copper, was once a popular standard in England, particularly before the early 20th century when the British hallmarking laws changed. This alloy offered a middle ground between the affordability of lower carat golds and the high purity and richness of 18-carat gold. It was widely utilized in Victorian England for making various types of jewellery, including brooches, rings, and pendants, prized for its durability and richer colour compared to 12-carat gold. The unique historical context of 15-carat gold gives it a special appeal, particularly among collectors and enthusiasts of antique jewellery today, serving as a cherished link to the past and a testament to the era's craftsmanship.

18 Carat Gold. 18c 18k 18ct 750

18 carat gold, comprising 75% pure gold, offers a significant upgrade in gold content and value compared to 9 carat gold. This makes it considerably more expensive to buy and valuable when selling. It can be found in the UK and frequently abroad, such as in Italy and other EU countries. Similar to other gold types, it is available in yellow, white (rhodium plated), and rose (copper added) varieties. It is identified by the hallmark number "18" or "750," indicating 750 parts gold per 1,000. This high-carat gold strikes a balance between purity and durability, being hard enough for practical use while showcasing the rich, lustrous quality of high-purity gold. Buyers should be cautious of foreign 18 carat gold hallmarks, as some may not adhere strictly to purity standards, necessitating scientific testing for accuracy, especially if the hallmark is not clearly defined.

18 carat Gold is both sold in Europe and in the UK. Look for the full UK hallmarks (see section on hallmarking below) Examine whether the hallmark is rough or not. Valued at twice the price of 9 carat gold extreme care should be taken when testing (see section__ and valuing see section this type of gold. A mistake would be costly and there are many fake "750" marks around in the marketplace right now.

22 Carat Gold. 22c 22ct 22k 916

22 carat gold is a high-purity gold alloy containing 91.6% gold, making it softer and more malleable than lower carat golds. It is a popular choice for wedding rings and gold coins, including Sovereigns and half sovereigns. This gold type is also prevalent in Asian jewellery, although it is essential to ensure proper hallmarking due to instances of sub-standard purity in some Asian gold. The hallmark number "22" or "916" indicates its purity of 916 parts per 1,000. While 22 carat gold has more than twice the gold content of 9 carat gold and is significantly more expensive, it is softer and less suitable for items subject to heavy wear. It is available in yellow, white (rhodium plated), and rose (copper added) varieties. As with other high-carat golds, it is crucial to verify the accuracy of foreign hallmarks, especially from regions without strict hallmarking laws.

You should be aware that gold UK coins are normally 22carat gold for example, Sovereigns, half-sovereigns, guineas etc. As regards jewellery etc 22 carat gold can be found in wedding rings (very popular at one time) and more rarely chains pendants etc. A lot of Asian gold can also be 22 carat gold, but then again it can vary wildly, so Asian jewellery is best avoided until more experienced.

24 Carat Gold 999, 24ct, 24k

24 carat gold is the purest form of gold available, with a composition of 99.9% gold, making it extremely soft and flexible. This gold is primarily used in high-value investment pieces rather than everyday jewellery due to its softness. It is easily identified by the hallmark "999," representing 999 parts of gold per 1,000. While 24 carat gold's high purity gives it a distinctive, rich yellow colour, its malleability makes it less practical for items that require durability. To get a price for your 24-carat gold, you can use a gold and precious metals price calculator to ensure an accurate valuation.

Pure gold is rare in jewellery. The mark 999, found in jewellery from Hong Kong is the closest you will get, but 24 carat gold it is found far more commonly in bullion bars and coins for example Britannias, maples, pandas and so on. These are relatively easy buys but always check purity and weight see chapter ---- Stick to named bars from recognised manufacturers e.g. PAMP Suisse Johnson Matthey Credit Suisse Perth Mint Royal Canadian Mint Valcambi Engelhard Argor-Heraeus Sunshine Minting The Royal Mint Rand Refinery Metalor Asahi Refining Baird & Co. Heraeus Umicore.

WARNING

Fake hallmarks on jewellery and fake coins and bars are commonplace these days . Look for rough looking hallmarks for signs of forgery. In regard to bars and coins check both purities and weights . These points are covered several times in the following chapters.

Silver

Silver is dealt with as a buyer in terms of its purity, but here we do not talk about carats, we instead use percentage purity in parts out of 1000 i.e. 500/1000 or 925/1000. The most common silver purities are;

500/1000 Silver or 50% Silver

500/1000 Silver, also known as 50% Silver, is a significant alloy in the history of coinage, particularly in the United Kingdom. From 1920 to 1946, British silver coins were minted using this purity, marking a transitional period from the higher silver content coins of the past to the lower silver content coins that followed. This alloy consists of 50% pure silver and 50% other metals, typically copper, giving it a balanced combination of durability and silver content. Although less valuable in terms of silver content compared to higher purities, 500/1000 Silver coins hold substantial historical and collectible value. Besides the UK, this silver alloy is occasionally found in coins from other countries, adding to its international numismatic interest. The use of 500/1000 Silver reflects economic and resource considerations of the time, making it an important aspect of 20th-century monetary history.

Warning

Silver gilt or vermeil, looks like gold, but it is actually a microscopically thin layer of gold over silver and due to the difficulty of separation, is always treated as silver.

Besides gold you should be looking for silver and 50% silver coins are a relatively easy buy as they are rarely faked Look for silver UK coins of any denomination /value between these dates, on markets, fairs boot sales etc.

800 Silver

800 Silver, also known as Continental Silver, is a widely recognized standard across Europe. This alloy contains 80% pure silver and 20% other metals, usually copper, which imparts additional strength and durability to the metal. This composition has made 800 Silver a popular choice for a variety of items, including jewellery, tableware, and decorative objects. The alloy's balance of beauty and robustness makes it ideal for everyday use and artistic applications. In some instances, particularly in Europe, 800 Silver can also be found in higher purities such as 900 Silver. The distinction between these grades lies in their silver content, with 900 Silver containing 90% pure silver, offering even greater value and lustre. Both 800 and 900 Silver have played significant roles in European craftsmanship and coinage, underscoring the region's rich tradition of metalwork and design.

800 silver marks i.e. 800 are widely faked on the Continent so testing is essential (please read Chapter 3 Look also for give-away signs like copper coming through the silver and of course the quality of the stamp. A rough hallmark is a give-away.

900 Silver

Besides the commonly known 800 Silver, 900 Silver is another prevalent form of silver alloy, widely used across the continent of Europe. This higher purity silver, composed of 90% silver and 10% other metals, often copper, is esteemed for its increased durability and attractive sheen, making it a preferred choice for a variety of applications. Notably, 900 Silver holds significant historical and cultural value as it has been the standard for many American silver coins. Prior to the introduction of the modern pure silver bullion coins, the United States Mint extensively used 900 Silver for its coinage, including iconic coins such as the Morgan and Peace dollars. This blend provided a balance between aesthetic appeal and practical durability, essential for everyday currency. Today, collectors and enthusiasts highly prize 900 Silver coins for their historical significance and intrinsic value. In addition to its numismatic uses, 900 Silver is also commonly found in fine jewellery, tableware, and decorative items, where its lustrous finish and substantial feel continue to be appreciated by artisans and consumers alike.

Much the same as for 800 silver though you will also come across US currency which is 900 silver. Do the same tests as for 800 silver.

925 or Sterling Silver

925 Silver, more commonly known as Sterling Silver, is one of the most well-known and widely used silver alloys in the world. Consisting of 92.5% pure silver and 7.5% other metals, typically copper, Sterling Silver offers an excellent balance of purity and strength. This composition enhances the metal's durability without significantly compromising its lustrous appearance, making it ideal for a wide range of applications. Sterling Silver has been the standard for fine silver jewellery, cutlery, and decorative objects for centuries. Its hallmark, often stamped as "925," is a mark of quality and authenticity recognized globally. The alloy's popularity stems from its beautiful sheen, ease of workability, and resistance to tarnishing when properly cared for. Whether in the form of intricate jewellery pieces, elegant tableware, or treasured heirlooms, Sterling Silver continues to be a preferred choice for artisans and consumers alike, embodying a rich tradition of craftsmanship and timeless beauty.

Sterling silver is the most common type of silver found in the UK often with full UK hallmarks. But the mark 925 is universally common as is the same purity as UK sterling silver. Many fakes are present in the marketplace especially from Mexico so test every piece that does not have a full UK hallmark. Many pieces are also filled with lead, resin and plaster of paris including vase bases, boxes, ornaments and figurines (Please see below)

958 Silver (Britannia Silver)

Britannia silver refers to a high-grade silver alloy first introduced in Britain in 1697 to replace sterling silver as the mandatory standard for items like plates, vessels, and coins. Containing 95.84% silver, compared to the 92.5% in sterling, Britannia silver is distinguished by its higher purity, resulting in a softer and more richly detailed finished product, ideal for intricate craftsmanship. The hallmark for Britannia silver features the figure of Britannia, which helped to differentiate it from sterling silver items marked with a lion passant. Although the use of Britannia silver was initially legislated to prevent coin clipping, its unique properties have made it a favoured material for fine silverware and collectible items, particularly appealing to those who value superior quality and detailed silver craft. Not as common as sterling silver.

999 Silver

999 Silver, also known as Fine Silver or Pure Silver, represents the highest purity of silver available, containing 99.9% pure silver with minimal trace elements. This nearly perfect composition gives 999 Silver its characteristic soft and lustrous quality, making it highly sought after for investment purposes, particularly in the form of bullion coins and bars. Fine Silver's superior purity makes it less suitable for everyday use items like jewellery or tableware, as it is relatively soft and prone to scratching and deformation. However, its unparalleled purity makes it ideal for certain industrial applications, such as in electronics and high-precision equipment, where conductivity and corrosion resistance are paramount. In the world of numismatics and precious metals investment, 999 Silver holds a prestigious position, often minted into coins and bars that serve both as legal tender and as a hedge against economic uncertainty. Collectors and investors value 999 Silver for its intrinsic value, purity, and the prestige associated with owning such a high-grade precious metal.

Silver bars and coins are made out of pure silver usually and are relatively easy to buy and sell, being bullion coins/bars. Named bars e.g. Pamp and Umicore etc are the safest bet as they have serial numbers and harder to fake. But again, always test. Manufacturers include PAMP Suisse Johnson Matthey Credit Suisse Perth Mint Royal Canadian Mint Valcambi Engelhard Argor-Heraeus Sunshine Minting The Royal Mint Rand Refinery Metalor Asahi Refining Baird & Co. Heraeus Umicore

Filled Silver Items

Many silver items, including 800/900 and sterling silver objects can be filled. They could have weighted bases or filled from top to bottom. Always check by using snips to cut into any part of the item you believe to be filled before buying items like these include vases, candlesticks, boxes, cases, pens, silver ornaments figurines etc is far less than you might imagine. Then there are also silver fakes. I will explore more on this in the following chapters.

Platinum

Platinum is a precious metal known for its exceptional durability, rarity, and distinctive silver-white lustre. It is widely used in jewellery, coins, and industrial applications. Platinum can be found in various purities, most notably 999, 950, and 800.

999 Platinum:

This is the purest form of platinum, containing 99.9% pure platinum. It is primarily used in platinum bullion coins and bars for investment purposes. The hallmark "999" signifies its purity of 999 parts per 1,000. Due to its high purity, 999 platinum is highly valued and sought after by investors.

950 Platinum:

This alloy contains 95% pure platinum and 5% other metals, usually iridium or ruthenium, which enhance its hardness and durability. 950 platinum is the standard for fine jewellery, including rings, necklaces, bracelets, and other high-end pieces. The hallmark "950" indicates its purity. Platinum's resistance to tarnish and corrosion makes it ideal for everyday wear, retaining its beauty over time.

800 Platinum:

This alloy consists of 80% pure platinum and 20% other metals. While less common, it is used in some jewellery and industrial applications where additional strength is needed. The hallmark "800" indicates its purity of 800 parts per 1,000.

Beyond its use in jewellery and investment, platinum plays a crucial role in the automotive industry. It is a key component in catalytic converters, which help reduce harmful emissions from vehicles. The catalytic properties of platinum enable it to convert toxic gases like carbon monoxide and hydrocarbons into less harmful substances, making it essential for meeting environmental standards.

Platinum that is hallmarked is safe to buy but steer clear of unhallmarked pieces.

Palladium

Palladium is a lustrous, silvery-white metal that shares many properties with platinum, including its use in jewellery, coins, and industrial applications. Palladium can be found in different purities, notably 999 and 950.

999 Palladium:

This is the purest form of palladium, containing 99.9% pure palladium. It is primarily used in palladium bullion coins and bars for investment purposes. The hallmark "999" signifies its high purity, making it highly valued by investors and collectors.

950 Palladium:

This alloy contains 95% pure palladium and 5% other metals, typically ruthenium or other platinum group metals. 950 palladium is widely used in fine jewellery, offering a durable and hypoallergenic option. The hallmark "950" indicates its purity. Palladium's bright white finish and resistance to tarnish make it a popular choice for wedding bands and other jewellery items.

500 palladium

500 palladium is an alloy that consists of 50% palladium, combined with other metals like silver or copper to enhance durability and workability. Known for its natural white lustre that resembles platinum but at a lower cost, 500 palladium is particularly valued in the jewellery industry for rings, necklaces, and watches. Its hypoallergenic properties make it suitable for wearers with sensitive skin, and its robustness allows for everyday use. This alloy is a popular choice for those seeking a platinum-like appearance without the higher expense, making it an attractive option for both contemporary and traditional jewellery designs.

In addition to its use in jewellery and investment, palladium is also critical in the automotive industry. Like platinum, palladium is used in catalytic converters to reduce vehicle emissions. Its ability to convert harmful gases into less toxic substances makes it an essential component for meeting environmental regulations and improving air quality.

Both platinum and palladium are also used in various high-tech applications, including electronics, dentistry, and chemical processing, due to their unique properties and catalytic abilities.

Palladium that is hallmarked is safe to buy but steer clear of unhallmarked pieces.

Gold-Filled, Rolled Gold, Gold and Silver Plated

No book on this subject would be complete without mentioning Gold-Filled, Rolled Gold-, Gold- and Silver-Plated items. These items are worth far less than actual gold and silver-plated items have little value and are best avoided when starting out You will find that it is easy to mistakenly identify rolled gold or gold-filled as actual gold.

Gold-Filled Jewellery

Gold-filled jewellery is a type of jewellery that consists of a solid layer of gold, typically constituting at least 5% of the item's total weight, mechanically bonded to a base metal or sterling silver. This process involves high pressure and heat to fuse the gold layer onto the core metal, creating a durable and high-quality product. The terms "rolled gold plate," "gold overlay," and "gold-filled" are often used interchangeably. However, "rolled gold plate" usually refers to items where the gold layer constitutes less than 5% of the item's weight but is still thicker than standard gold plating.

High-quality gold-filled pieces have the same appearance as high-carat gold and are known for their longevity. Even with daily wear, gold-filled jewellery can last between 10 to 30 years, though eventually, the gold layer will wear off, exposing the underlying metal. The gold layer on gold-filled items is significantly thicker than that on regular gold-plated jewellery —5 to 10 times thicker—and 15 to 25 times thicker than that produced by gold electroplating. Items marked with "HGE" (heavy gold electroplate) or "HGP" (heavy gold plate) often indicate gold plating, but these marks lack legal significance and only suggest the item is gold plated.

Gold-filled and rolled gold jewellery is often marked with specific hallmarks to indicate its composition and quality. Common marks include:

1. "1/20 14K GF" indicating the gold layer is 1/20th the total weight and is 14 karat gold.
2. "G.F" or "gf" standing for gold-filled.
3. "R.G.P" or "rolled gold plate" indicating a rolled gold

item.

4. Terms like "metal core" or "bronze core" indicating the base metal used.

5. "Front & back" or "f & bk" indicating that both sides of the item are gold-filled or rolled gold.

Gold Plating

Gold plating is a method of depositing a thin layer of gold onto the surface of another metal, often copper or silver (creating silver-gilt), through chemical or electrochemical plating processes. This technique is commonly used in the modern electronics industry to enhance the conductivity and resistance to corrosion of electronic components. Traditional methods of gold plating, often referred to as gilding, are used for much larger objects and decorative items.

The gold layer produced by gold plating is much thinner than that of gold-filled or rolled gold jewellery. Gold-plated items have a layer of gold that can wear off relatively quickly, especially with frequent use. Marks to look out for when identifying gold-plated items include:

1. "1/5th metal core" indicating a specific proportion of the core metal.
2. "G.F" or "gf" for gold-filled, though often misinterpreted as gold plated.
3. "R.G.P" for rolled gold plate.
4. "Metal core" or "bronze core" indicating the base metal used.
5. "Front & back" or "f & bk" suggesting both sides are plated.

Gold electroplating, sometimes stamped "HGE" (heavy gold electroplate) or "HGP" (heavy gold plate), involves a process where a thin layer of gold is electrically deposited onto the surface of the base metal. Despite the name, these marks do not have legal standing and only indicate that the item has a gold layer, which is significantly thinner compared to gold-filled or rolled gold items.

Silver-Plated Items

Silver-plated items are similar to gold-plated items, where a thin layer of silver is deposited onto a base metal, usually copper or brass. Silver plating is often used for tableware, decorative objects, and jewellery to provide the appearance of solid silver at a lower cost. The process involves electroplating, where the base metal is submerged in a solution containing silver ions and an electric current is applied to deposit a thin layer of silver onto the surface.

Silver-plated items can vary in quality based on the thickness of the silver layer and the base metal used. Marks to identify silver-plated items include:

1. "EP" or "EPNS" indicating electroplated nickel silver.
2. "Silver on copper" indicating a copper core.
3. "Sheffield plate" for a specific method of silver plating.

Both gold-filled, rolled gold, and silver-plated jewellery offer more affordable alternatives to solid gold or silver jewellery, each with its own characteristics and durability. Understanding the differences between these types of jewellery and their markings can help consumers make informed purchasing decisions.

When starting out as a gold dealer it is vital to always check whether any type of gold you are viewing is actually silver gilt, rolled gold or gold plate or gold-filled Proper testing see Chapter 3 can help you avoid costly errors Many experienced gold buyers buy this type of metal for a fraction of the cost of actual gold and tend to recover the gold from the base metal in a variety of ways This often proves uneconomical due to the costs of various acids e.g. HCL, H2SO4 and Aqua regia PLUS many gold processors pay far less than the actual carat achieved due to higher processing costs

Without an organized large-scale process trying to recover gold from rolled gold is a waste of time, but all gold dealers when first setting out are often tricked by a piece of rolled gold so testing is essential.

Always remember that you can plate a bedroom floor in area size with less than an ounce of gold, The following marks indicate better quality of plating, better for gold recovery but are still hard to sell in the trade so best avoided.

1/ 1/5th metal core (after years of wear often end up closer to $1/20^{th}$ gold)

3/ "metal core" or "bronze core" (same as above)

4/ "Front & back" or "f & bk." (same as above)

As regards silver-plated items, forget them. They have little metal value and uneconomical to process but be careful with the hallmarks as they often look like silver hallmarks until viewed closely.

Silver Gilt

As regards silver gilt items These can also be called gold or silver or bonded gold. It's another potential trap but most of these items are marked with a silver lion passant mark or the numbers 925.

Hallmarking & Gold Carats

NB UK hallmarks are dealt with first, followed by hallmarking of different countries

In the realm of gold trading and jewelry making, hallmarking is a critical process that guarantees the purity and authenticity of gold items. In the UK, the responsibility for hallmarking lies with the Assay Office, an independent entity that rigorously tests items submitted by jewelers to ensure they meet the stringent purity standards required for a hallmark. Unlike some European countries where jewelers may apply hallmarks themselves, in the UK, the hallmark serves as an independent verification that an item has been tested and confirmed to contain the gold content claimed.

This system of certification helps protect consumers from fraud and ensures that the gold market maintains high standards of honesty and quality. Any gold item that should bear a hallmark but does not is automatically suspect, as the absence of a hallmark generally indicates that the item has not met the necessary standards of purity. For those entering the business of buying and selling gold, it is advised to trade primarily in hallmarked items to avoid the risks associated with unverified gold. This approach not only safeguards the dealer's investment but also builds trust with customers, establishing a reputation for dealing in high-quality, authenticated gold.

Internationally, hallmarking practices can vary significantly. Many countries have their own systems and standards, which may not always match the rigor of the UK's. In places like India and China, hallmarking has become more regulated in recent years, with efforts to align more closely with global standards to facilitate international trade. However, in other regions, hallmarking may still be less strict or enforced, making it crucial for buyers and sellers to be particularly vigilant when dealing with international transactions. Understanding the hallmarking requirements and the reliability of hallmarking institutions in each country is essential for anyone involved in the global gold market.

COMPULSORY MARKS	THE HALLMARK COMPRISES THREE COMPULSORY MARKS: A SPONSOR'S MARK, A FINENESS MARK AND AN ASSAY OFFICE MARK.				
Sponsor's Mark The registered mark of the company that submitted the article for hallmarking.	Fineness Mark Tells you the precious metal content, expressed in parts per thousand				Assay Office Mark Tells you which Assay Office tested and hallmarked the article.
	Silver	Palladium	Gold	Platinum	
A B	800	2009 500	375 9 carat	850	London
	925 Sterling	950	585 14 carat	900	Birmingham
	958 Britannia	999	750 18 carat	950	Sheffield
	999	2010 500	916 22 carat	999	Edinburgh
		950	990		
		999	999		
OPTIONAL MARKS	YOU MAY SEE OPTIONAL MARKS, SUCH AS THE TRADITIONAL FINENESS SYMBOL AND THE DATE LETTER DEPICTING THE YEAR THE ITEM WAS HALLMARKED.				
Traditional Fineness Symbols	Sterling Silver	Sterling Silver Scotland	Britannia Silver	Palladium	Gold	Platinum
Date Letter	j 2008	k 2009	l 2010	m 2011	n 2012	o 2013
International Convention Marks	925 Silver	950 Palladium	375 Gold	950 Platinum	This mark is used by countries, including the United Kingdom, that are signatories to the International Convention on Hallmarking and is recognised by all those countries
Exemption Weights* Articles above these weights must be hallmarked	7.78 grams	1.0 gram	1.0 gram	0.5 grams	

UK hallmarked gold is not an issue as the Assay office test every part of every gold jewellery item and when satisfied that the gold, whether it is 9 carat,18 carat, 22 carat Gold, sets the rigorous requirement on all parts of the tested gold item, they give a full hallmark. **Hallmarking differs around the world** It is an offence for a retailer to sell any product made of gold, silver or platinum in the UK unless it has been hallmarked.

Current Legislation

ELIZABETH II

Hallmarking Act 1973

1973 CHAPTER 43

An Act to make fresh provision for the composition, assaying, marking and description of articles of, or containing, precious metals, and as to approvals for the implementation and enforcement thereof; and for purposes connected with those matters. [25th July 1973]

BE IT ENACTED by the Queen's most Excellent Majesty, by and with the advice and consent of the Lords Spiritual and Temporal, and Commons, in this present Parliament assembled, and by the authority of the same, as follows:—

1.—(1) Subject to the provisions of this Act, any person who, in the course of a trade or business—

(a) applies to an unhallmarked article a description indicating that it is wholly or partly made of gold, silver or platinum, or

(b) supplies, or offers to supply, an unhallmarked article to which such a description is applied,

shall be guilty of an offence.

(2) Subsection (1) above shall not apply to a description which is permitted by Part I of Schedule 1 to this Act

(3) Subsection (1) above shall not apply to an article within Part II of the said Schedule.

(4) Notwithstanding section 3(2) of the Trade Descriptions Act 1968 (definition of " false trade description " as one which is false to a material degree) a trade description which indicates the fineness (whether in parts per thousand or otherwise) of any

A 1

1973 The Hallmarking Act

The 1973 Hallmarking Act was the culmination of a very lengthy and complex process involving over 30 statutes relating to hallmarking, some of which had been adjusted or partly repealed. Many included requirements inappropriate to the new economic and social situation. An overhaul of legislation was well overdue. Eventually the Hallmarking Act 1973 was passed, championed by Jerry Wiggin MP, a descendant of a Birmingham family associated with the Assay Office for generations.

The new Act created the British Hallmarking Council,

harmonised date letters, simplified gold standards and reinforced compulsory hallmarking for gold, silver and, for the first time, platinum.

Nowhere else in the world are consumers more highly protected than in the UK. The UK is one of only a few countries in the world that have compulsory statutory hallmarking. This means that every item sold as precious metal, i.e. gold, silver, platinum or palladium must have been tested and hallmarked by an independent third-party Assay Office to guarantee that the precious metal is of the fineness stated.

The law applies to everything SOLD in the UK, regardless of where it may have been manufactured. The only exemptions are items which fall beneath the specified weight thresholds which are 1 gram for gold, 7.78 grams for silver, 0.5 grams for platinum and 1 gram for palladium.

Hallmarking in the USA, EU, and Other International Regions

Hallmarking, the practice of stamping precious metal objects with marks that indicate their purity and authenticity, is a crucial part of the jewelry and precious metals industries worldwide. While the UK has one of the most stringent and long-established hallmarking systems, other regions, including the USA, the European Union, and various countries around the world, have their own approaches to hallmarking. Below is an overview of how hallmarking operates in the USA, the EU, and other key international markets.

1. Hallmarking in the USA

In the United States, hallmarking practices differ significantly from those in countries with government-regulated systems, such as the UK. Rather than being controlled by state-run assay offices, hallmarking in the USA is largely regulated by the Federal Trade Commission (FTC) through its Guides for the Jewelry, Precious Metals, and Pewter Industries. These guidelines outline rules for marking and advertising precious metals, including gold, silver, platinum, and palladium.

Voluntary Hallmarking: In the U.S., hallmarking is not mandatory by law, but manufacturers and jewelers voluntarily mark items to ensure consumer trust and transparency.

Legal Requirements: Products must be stamped with both the metal purity (e.g., "14K" for 14 karat gold) and the manufacturer's or distributor's trademark. If a precious metal is alloyed with another metal, the alloy's presence must also be clearly indicated.

Karats for Gold: U.S. law allows a range of gold purity stamps such as 10K, 14K, and 18K, which indicate the proportion of pure gold in the alloy (10/24ths, 14/24ths, etc.).

While the U.S. does not have official assay offices, manufacturers rely on third-party laboratories and organizations, such as Jewelers of America (JA), for quality assurance and testing.

2. Hallmarking in the European Union

In the European Union, hallmarking practices are more varied due to the number of member states, each with its own traditions and laws. However, some degree of harmonization has occurred thanks to the Vienna Convention on the Control and Marking of Precious Metals, which many EU nations have ratified.

Vienna Convention: This international treaty establishes standards for hallmarking precious metals across participating countries. Member countries include Austria, France, Italy, the Netherlands, Portugal, and Spain, among others. The convention defines hallmarking requirements such as purity marks, the assay office stamp, and manufacturer identification.

Hallmarking Offices: Several EU countries maintain state-controlled assay offices similar to those in the UK. For example, France and Spain have longstanding assay systems where all precious metal items must be tested and marked before being sold.

Optional in Some Countries: In countries like Germany and Italy, hallmarking is not mandatory, but voluntary marks are often used. Manufacturers may submit their items for testing and certification by independent labs or assay offices.

Hallmarks in the EU often include a purity mark (e.g., 925 for sterling silver), the assay office mark, and a responsibility mark identifying the maker or importer.

3. Hallmarking in Other Regions

Beyond the USA and the EU, hallmarking systems vary widely across the globe, with different levels of regulation, enforcement, and traditions.

India: In India, hallmarking has become more regulated since the government made hallmarking of gold jewelry compulsory in 2021. The Bureau of Indian Standards (BIS) oversees the hallmarking process, which includes marking jewelry with purity levels such as 22K, 18K, and 14K, as well as a BIS mark, the jeweler's identification, and a year of marking.

China: In China, hallmarking is overseen by the China National Accreditation Service for Conformity Assessment (CNAS), which is responsible for testing and certifying the purity of precious metals. Items are generally marked with a standard purity level (e.g., 999 for pure gold) and may include other details like the manufacturer's mark.

Japan: Japan uses a voluntary hallmarking system for precious metals, and hallmarks typically consist of the karat or purity number and the symbol of the responsible manufacturer or distributor. The system is regulated by the Japan Mint and focuses primarily on consumer trust and transparency.

4. Global Harmonization and Mutual Recognition
Despite the varied hallmarking systems worldwide, efforts have been made to harmonize standards across borders. The International Hallmarking Convention (under the Vienna Agreement) is one such effort, allowing for mutual recognition of hallmarks between signatory countries. This reduces the need for re-assaying and re-marking items that are sold

internationally, which simplifies trade in precious metals.

Countries that adhere to the Vienna Convention apply a common control mark (CCM), which assures that items meet the minimum legal purity requirements, regardless of where they are sold. This international system benefits consumers and businesses by promoting transparency and consistency in the global precious metals market.

5. Key Takeaways

The USA has a voluntary hallmarking system governed by the FTC, with no official assay offices.

The EU has a diverse hallmarking system, with some countries having mandatory state-regulated marks and others allowing voluntary hallmarking.

Countries like India, China, and Japan have developed their own hallmarking systems, with increasing regulation in response to consumer demand for authenticity.

Global efforts like the Vienna Convention promote mutual recognition of hallmarks, fostering international trade in precious metals.

Hallmarking systems around the world are evolving to meet consumer expectations for transparency and quality assurance. Whether mandatory or voluntary, hallmarking plays a crucial role in maintaining trust in the jewelry and precious metals industries across different regions.

Chapter 2 Summary: Gold, Silver, Platinum & Palladium – Weights, Carats & Purities

Chapter 2 provides a detailed overview of the different measurements and standards used to assess the purity and weight of precious metals, including gold, silver, platinum, and palladium. It discusses the units of measurement specific to the industry, such as grams and troy ounces, and explains the carat system used to describe gold purity. Additionally, the chapter highlights the significance of hallmarking in determining the authenticity and quality of precious metals.

Key Points:
Measurement Units:

Grams: The primary unit for measuring precious metals, where one gram is one-thousandth of a kilogram.
Troy Ounce vs. Ounce (Avoirdupois): A troy ounce (31.1035 grams) is used specifically in the precious metals market and differs from the avoirdupois ounce (28.3495 grams) typically used in cooking. Understanding these differences is crucial for accurate valuation and trading.
Carats and Purities:

Gold Purity: Measured in carats, where 24 carat signifies pure gold. Lower carats indicate gold mixed with other metals, which enhances durability but reduces purity.
Common Gold Carats: Includes 9 carat (37.5% gold), 14 carat (58.5% gold), 18 carat (75% gold), and 22 carat (91.6% gold), each marked with specific codes like 375, 585, 750, and 916 respectively.
Platinum and Palladium: Also measured in similar purity standards, with common marks like 950 (95% pure) for jewelry-quality platinum.
Hallmarking:

Importance of Hallmarks: Hallmarks are crucial for verifying the purity of precious metals, acting as a certification that the item meets established purity standards.

UK Hallmarking: Stringent and regulated by law, ensuring that all precious metal items sold are tested and marked by independent assay offices.

Global Differences: Hallmarking standards can vary significantly between countries, impacting the reliability of purity assessments in international markets.

Legislation and Standards:

1973 Hallmarking Act: Centralized and updated the UK's hallmarking regulations, setting high consumer protection standards and making it illegal to sell unmarked precious metal items.

Assay Offices: Play a critical role in testing and certifying the purity of gold, silver, platinum, and palladium pieces.

Takeaway Points:

Understanding Weights and Measures: Proficiency in using grams and troy ounces is essential for anyone involved in the buying, selling, or trading of precious metals.

Recognizing Carat Purity: Knowing the carat system helps in assessing the value and quality of gold. Higher carats indicate greater purity but also increased softness and susceptibility to wear.

Importance of Hallmarking: Hallmarks are not just marks of purity but are essential for legal trading in markets like the UK. They serve as a safeguard for both buyers and sellers.

Necessity of Accurate Testing: Due to variations in hallmarking laws globally, it is crucial to verify the authenticity of precious metal items, especially when dealing with international goods or older pieces where hallmarks might not be as standardized.

This chapter equips readers with the fundamental knowledge needed to navigate the complexities of the precious metals market, emphasizing the critical role of accurate measurement and rigorous testing to maintain trust and integrity in trading practices.

CHAPTER 3 TESTING & WEIGHING GOLD & SILVER

The need to practice.

Before you actually sit in front of a customer you will need a good understanding of how to test gold and silver and identify purities. This will of course need practice and I advise you to practice on any gold or silver scrap you may have lying around, or on any old unwanted jewellery and or coins . You will not be affecting the scrap value.

You will have seen that you will need scales and a loupe. Here is a list of all the things that you will need to become a gold buyer.

Requirements for testing & Weighing.

1/ Set of Scales

These should be available to measure gram weight and should be able to weigh at least 1000g. Trading standards calibrated scales are used by many gold buyers these days at a cost of around £300. Ensure every time you use you start with a "0" i.e. tare scales properly and always check that you are weighing in grams not ounces, not grains etc.

2/ Eye Glass/loupe

10x magnification is the one to go for here. Avoid oversize loupes as these can prevent you from getting close enough to read small hallmarks. If you are going to be buying diamonds, then a 20x magnification loupe may also be required.

3/ Acid and file. The next chapter covers testing and both acid and a file will be required. Acid sets can be bought from jewellery suppliers e.g. Cooksons, but as we will see later, 9ct acid is the primary acid you will be using. Look to spend around £60 for acid with a needle file, important for scratching into items to apply the acid.

4/ Calculator. Invest in a simple but reliable calculator, preferably one that also does percentages. Cost £20

5/ Magnet. A powerful neodymium magnet will pick out any ferrous based non-gold or non-silver metal when testing jewellery. A must have for any gold buyer Cost £30 max.

6/ Diamond tester. Whilst this is not required at the outset, it can be useful when being presented with rings with stones. The tester will help identify a diamond ring, which will have more value than scrap, but will also help you identify which rings with stones are actually scrap. For example, CZs i.e. cubic zirconias have little value and are normally treated as scrap. A diamond tester such as the Dymond tester costs £240

7/ XRF analyser.

These extremely accurate machines cost upwards of £18,000 for a good one, so most likely well out of budget for anyone starting out in the business SO, find a gold buyer(possibly one you can and will sell to0 and offer to pay when you need the odd item tested but NB a c\void

8/ A good pair of snips .

These are essential both in the buying and the selling process. You will be using them to break into filled gold items e.g. bangles, or for removing non gold metal from jewellery pieces. They will also be used to crack out worthless stones. When selling all your gold will have to be cleaned (see later chapters) and again your snips will be invaluable. Hammerheads are probably the best to use here. These are essential both in the buying and the selling process.

Avoid There are a range of cheap testers on the market that purport to identify carats etc e.g. the Mizar. These are inaccurate and are to be avoided.

Other bits and pieces you will need will be a PC for giving receipts etc, a hard copy of the hallmark chart which can be obtained from any assay office and of course the usual office paraphernalia, pens, paper, copier etc.

Armed with the knowledge you have read so far and with the necessary tools of the trade is, you are ready to start buying gold and silver.

The process of Testing & Weighing

In this day and age many of the larger gold buyers use XRF analysis to test items. X-ray fluorescence (XRF) is a non-destructive analytical technique used to determine the composition of gold and other precious metals. This method involves exposing the sample to a beam of X-rays, which causes the elements within the sample to emit fluorescent X-rays of their own. By measuring the energy and intensity of these fluorescent X-rays, XRF can accurately identify and quantify the elements present in the sample, including the gold content. This makes XRF an invaluable tool for verifying the purity of gold items quickly and precisely without damaging them, widely used by jewellers, bullion dealers, and assay offices. These instruments whether hand-held or desktop cost £15000 upwards. As a gold dealer starting out you may well not be able to afford one but there is one thing you can do about that, as detailed in chapter 4. Find a friendly gold buyer and ask if he would test pieces for you. Offer to pay as these machines are not cheap and have high maintenance.

Now we are ready to test.

Step 1 Eyes & Loupe

Carefully examine every millimetre of the item you are considering buying. You are looking for anything suspiciously not gold. For example, whilst a piece of rolled gold may seem to be real gold on a superficial examination, a careful close inspection could reveal base metal coming through. Check the quality of the hallmarks also. Always best to look closely, then rest your eyes for a second or two, then look again, forgetting everything but the item you are studying . Look at the gemstones as well. Any wear makes them scrap! Check also for filler in silver and gold items. Spinning fobs with stones often have filler in them and many silver items e.g. cutlery handles, candlesticks candelabra, boxes, ornaments and figurines are often filled with plaster of Paris, resin and some even have lead bases. Beware.

Step 2 Magnet

Wave the magnet around the item—any magnetism should immediately start alarm bells ringing. This could indicate the presence of a bit of solder, or it could mean the item has a metal wire running through it. This tends to apply mainly to bangles, which, if hallmarked, would be gold, but a metal wire might have been added for strength (so remember to deduct weight for the steel). Alternatively, it could mean the item is gold-plated, meaning no real gold content. If a ring, earring, pendant, or chain is magnetic, then it is not gold. If a bangle is magnetic, it could mean either that it is not gold, or it is gold with a metal wire running through it. A check of the hallmark will give you your answer.

Step 3: The Acid Test

For this, you will need to use your acid and a file.

Testing Acid

Warning : Acid is dangerous. Handle with care and follow all instructions for use. Do not breathe fumes.

A lot of gold buyers use a full acid test kit, but to start, all you will need is just 9-carat acid and a thin file. This will set you back around £30, and acid can be **bought from** jewellery supply companies such as Cooksons.

To test any gold or silver, you always have to file into the item to a depth of at least 1mm where possible. The deeper the mark, the more reliable the result. Carefully dab some 9-carat acid on the item and check for these results:

Brown: Filed area turns brown. This colour confirms that you have 9-carat gold, provided you have filed deep enough.

Lime Green with Fizz: This result means your item is not gold. The colour is obtained when the acid mixes with base metals like copper and zinc.

Grey: If the result is a grey colour, then your item is actually silver, most likely sterling silver. This is a great test for initially identifying silver, though further testing may be required.

No Reaction: This means that you have an item with a higher gold carat than nine carat, but it could also mean you have platinum or palladium.

More detailed Steps to Test Gold Using Acid

Acid testing is never 100% reliable but it is the best method around apart from XRF. There is also a lot of misinformation on the Internet. Just follow this simple guide.

1. Preparation:

i Clean the gold piece to remove any dirt or oils.

ii File a small notch in the piece to penetrate any surface plating and expose the underlying metal.

2. Testing with Acid:

9-Carat Acid Test

You've already tested with 9-carat acid and had a clear result, indicating the gold is at least 9 carats. BUT if there is NO reaction then you will need to test further

14/15-Carat Acid Test :

i Clean area again.

ii Apply a drop of 14/15-carat acid to the filed notch and observe the reaction:

Brown or green/brown: The gold is at least 14/15 carats.

No reaction : The gold will be higher than 14/15 carats. So, you will need to test again.

. 18-24 Carat/Platinum Acid Test

i Clean area again

ii Apply a drop of the higher carat acid (18k, 22k, or platinum) to the filed notch.

iii Observe the reaction:

Item turns yellow.

The slower the reaction usually the higher the carat . You might need to use your buyer's xrf to distinguish further e.g. between 20 and 24ct. The area tends to turn yellow quickly, almost immediately if it is 18 carat and slower for higher carats.

No reaction

item may well be platinum.

Tips for Accurate Testing

- Ensure the gold piece is clean and free of contaminants.

- File a notch to test the metal beneath any surface plating.

- Use a separate testing stone if you are testing multiple pieces to avoid cross-contamination.

- Wear gloves and safety glasses to protect yourself from the acids.

By following these steps and observing the reactions, you can accurately determine the purity of your gold piece.

Steps to Test Silver Using Silver Acid

1. Prepare the Surface:

- Clean the silver item thoroughly to remove any dirt, oils, or tarnish that could affect the test results.

- Use a non-abrasive cloth or a soft brush to clean the surface.

2. Make a Small Scratch:

- Use your jeweller's file or a testing stone to make a small, discreet scratch on the item. This exposes the underlying metal and ensures an accurate test by removing any plating or coating.

3. Apply the Acid:

- Place a drop of silver testing acid on the scratched area or on the testing stone where you have rubbed the item.

- Observe the colour change that occurs where the acid is applied.

4. Compare the Colour Change:

- Compare the resulting colour to the chart provided with your acid testing kit. Different purities of silver will react with the acid to produce specific colours.

Interpreting the Results

- Fine Silver (99.9% Pure):

The acid typically produces a very deep red colour.

Sterling Silver (92.5% Pure):

The acid usually turns a dark red or brownish-red colour, i.e. slightly lighter than for pure. Practice makes perfect.

Coin Silver (90% Pure):

The reaction often results in a light to medium red colour.

80% Silver:

- The colour change will be lighter red or pink.

- Low-Purity Silver:

- Lower purity silver or silver-plated items may not react strongly with the acid or could turn greenish, indicating the presence of base metals.

Safety Precautions

- Wear Protective Gear: Always wear gloves and safety goggles when handling acid to protect your skin and eyes from potential splashes.

- Work in a Ventilated Area: Perform the test in a well-ventilated space to avoid inhaling any fumes.

- Neutralize Spills: Keep a neutralizing solution, such as baking soda mixed with water, on hand to neutralize any acid spills immediately.

Conclusion

Silver acid testing is a straightforward and effective method for determining the purity of silver items. By following the correct procedure and safety precautions, you can accurately identify the fineness of silver, helping you make informed decisions about the value and authenticity of your silver pieces. Whether you are a jeweller, collector, or buyer, mastering this technique can be an invaluable skill in your toolkit.

Gold Coins & Bars

We have already established that there can be gold fakes about. Rough hallmarks can be dealt with by using acid, but gold coins and bars which are normally between 21 and 24 carat are much harder to verify using acid, not least because acid is unreliable between these carats. **BUT** you can also do further checks as follows.

i Google search the coin in question. This will give you valuable information such as weight diameter and purity.

ii weigh the coin. Allow a very small amount of weight loss if there is wear., The weight should be about right.

iii Check the diameter and measurements of the coin. Again, these should be correct.

if your coin does not pass this test e.g. for Sovereigns, Krugerrands Britannias etc then you have a fake coin, though often these can be made in gold albeit a lower carat than it should be.

With gold bars the process is similar, but dimensions may not be available . So

I Check the weight.

ii Check the quality of the stamping on the bar.

Iii If in doubt Don't gamble.

When testing any gold or silver, remember the following:

1. Handle all acids with care.

2. Wear gloves and eye protection.

3. Wipe any acid from the test area after testing.

Summary of Chapter 3: Testing and Weighing Gold & Silver

This chapter provides a comprehensive guide on the importance and methods of testing and weighing gold and silver. Emphasizing the need for practice, it advises practicing on scrap or unwanted jewellery to hone skills. The chapter details the necessary tools for a gold buyer and outlines the procedures for accurate testing and weighing. It includes the use of scales, loupes, acid tests, and magnets. Safety precautions are also highlighted to ensure safe handling of hazardous materials. The chapter aims to equip aspiring gold buyers with the knowledge and tools required for accurate assessment and valuation of precious metals.

Takeaway Points:

1. **Practice is Essential:**
   - Regularly practice on scrap gold, silver, and old jewellery to improve testing skills without affecting the item's scrap value.

2. **Essential Tools for Testing and Weighing:**
   - **Set of Scales:** Must measure in grams up to 1000g with trading standards calibration. Always tare to zero before use.

   - **Eye Glass/Loupe: 10x magnification for general use, 20x for diamonds. Avoid oversized loupes for better precision.**

- Acid and File: Necessary for testing metal purity. Use 9-carat acid primarily, and ensure you have a needle file for making test notches.

- Calculator: Simple, reliable, and capable of calculating percentages.

- Magnet: Neodymium magnet to detect non-gold or non-silver metals.

- Diamond Tester: Useful for identifying valuable stones versus scrap stones like cubic zirconias.

- XRF Analyser: Though expensive, it offers precise non-destructive testing. Partner with a gold buyer for occasional use.

- Snips: Essential for breaking into filled items and cleaning gold before selling.

3. Setting Up a Secure Workspace:
   - Consider renting a secure office or serviced office to establish a safe and professional environment for transactions.

4. Detailed Steps in Acid Testing:
   - **Preparation:** Clean the item thoroughly and file a small notch to expose the underlying metal.

   - **Testing with Acid:**

     - **Brown:** confirms 9-carat gold.

     - **Lime Green with Fizz:** Indicates the presence of base metals, not gold.

     - **Grey:** Likely sterling silver.

- **No Reaction:** Higher carat gold, platinum, or palladium.

5. **Further Acid Testing for Higher Carats:**
   - **14/15-Carat Acid Test:**

     - **Brown or green/brown** indicates 14/15 carat gold.

     - **No reaction** means higher than 14/15 carats.

   - **18-24 Carat/Platinum Acid Test:**

     - **Yellow** colour indicates high carat gold.

     - **No reaction** suggests platinum.

6. **Tips for Accurate Testing:**
   - Ensure the item is clean and contaminant-free.

   - **File a notch deep enough for accurate testing.**

   - **Use a separate testing stone for multiple items to avoid cross-contamination.**

   - **Always wear gloves and safety glasses during testing.**

7. **Testing Silver with Acid:**

   - **Preparation:** Clean the silver item and make a small scratch.

   - **Apply Acid:** Observe the colour change and compare to the chart provided with the testing kit.

- **Results Interpretation:**
  - **Fine Silver (99.9% Pure):** Very deep red colour.
  - **Sterling Silver (92.5% Pure):** Dark red or brownish-red colour.
  - **Coin Silver (90% Pure):** Light to medium red colour.
  - **80% Silver:** Lighter red or pink colour.
  - **Low-Purity Silver:** Greenish colour indicating base metals.

7. **Safety Precautions:**
   - Handle acids with care and follow all safety instructions.
   - **Always wear gloves and eye protection.**
   - **Work in a well-ventilated area and keep a neutralizing solution handy.**

8. **A word about Testing Gold Coins and Bars:**
   - **Gold Coins:** Verify authenticity by checking weight, diameter, and purity using Google search and measurements.
   - **Gold Bars: Check weight, stamping quality, and dimensions. Avoid gambling on unverified items.**

Conclusion

This chapter equips aspiring gold buyers with the foundational knowledge needed for accurate testing and weighing of precious metals. By mastering these techniques and following safety protocols, you can confidently assess the value of gold and silver items, ensuring profitable and secure transactions.

CHAPTER 4 SECURING YOUR BUYER

I said at the beginning of this book that all the best gold dealers I know have several traits in common as follows. That is *good* gold buyers by the way. There are plenty of rip-off merchants in the business also. Let's examine these points in more detail.

1/ They put the Customer First.

This is a standard trait of all good businesses. They identify your needs and satisfy them. Avoid rude, surly unhelpful gold buyers for obvious reasons. Find ones that go out of their way to assist you and particularly those willing to do a bit extra like provide you with free xrf testing on items you are unsure of.

2/ They are Honest

In this business honesty is required. Items should be weighed properly normally on trading standards calibrated scales, and the weights made visible to the seller. Prices should be clearly advertised and whilst the metal you will be selling should be cleaned from stones and dirt etc. unscrupulous gold buyers have a habit of knocking far too much weight off, so question any weight loss.

. Only use gold buyers that satisfy these criteria and never use any gold buyer that does not publish the prices they pay on their website/on premises. Check their reviews and what customers comment about them and watch out for one nasty little trick as follows …Some gold buyers show the LBMA spot price for gold and NOT the price they actually pay. Avoid at all costs!

3/ They are scrupulously careful and meticulous Good gold buyers carefully check every piece. Avoid companies that wave their hands over your items and offer a price for a job lot etc. This is both lazy on their part and could lead to you losing a small fortune. For your part and to help them work more efficiently make sure all non-gold (including pins on brooches, stones, wire in bangles etc. are all removed. This process can take some time and it is best if you try not to distract the gold buyer's concentration. Be empathetic as it is a high-pressure event, with often a lot of money in question.

4/ They do what they say, i.e. pay what they say they pay. We have already covered this but there are a few tricks to watch out for. Including knocking off too much weight for stones and non-metal parts as well as deliberately mis-identifying gold carats etc.

5/ They don't gamble on gold and silver purities etc.

If a good gold buyer is in doubt over an item, they will normally just "leave it out" i.e. pass on buying the item from you. They tend not to gamble and in the same way so must you not. So, if a gold buyer asks you to gamble on an item i.e. by saying "I am unsure will you take less, then don't gamble and get a second opinion.

Similarly, if you have a customer selling to you and you are unsure about an item, why not take it to your gold buyer to test for you., via Xrf, just give a receipt.

6/ They understand the metals and the math!

Walk quickly away from any gold dealer that can't identify carats properly, is hesitant or unsure or who keeps making silly maths errors.

7/ They are never greedy

Greed makes folk rush in. Be careful, avoid greed and pay a fair price But using a gold buyer that constantly pinches a few pounds from you here and there, every time you sell, with spurious excuses is a no-no Avoid.

So now we have a rough idea of what we are looking for. In basic terms, in this business you are looking to buy it at one price and sell it at another, higher price. So, before you start buying it from a variety of sources it is imperative to secure the source you are going to sell to….and that is before you go buying anything! This is the description of the buying process has been left to the next chapter.

In most countries of the world, gold buying is handled by private businesses. The small gold buyer like you, sells it on to a larger well-established gold buyer, who then sells it on to even larger gold processors with names like Umicore, Metalor. Who then refine the scrap back to pure gold in the EU. let's look at ways of finding your buyer.

Google Search

In the UK and Europe (US and Canada too) there are plenty of well-established gold buying businesses. For example, in the UK a quick Google search on the search terms "sell gold" or "gold buyers UK" reveal a whole host of companies like "Hatton Garden Metals", "The Birmingham Gold Company" "Scrapgolduk" "The London Gold Centre" and so on. The search term "list of Gold Buyers" also will yield results.

Take a look at their websites and disregard all those that do not post their buying prices exactly. Check their reviews especially Google reviews and read all the negative comments too. This will give you a good idea whom to use and who to reject.

Phone and/or Physical Visit

For those you have not rejected, it would be best to either telephone or call in, but whichever strategy is best for you, remember you are trying to build up a rapport with these well-established gold buyers, so a friendly approach is recommended.

A Word about KYC and AML

You are trying to establish whether they are prepared to take on another trade customer. There is no legal requirement that must be satisfied to become a gold dealer, but you will have to provide ID, proof of address and any forms pertaining to KYC (know your customer and AML (anti-money laundering regulations) and when you buy gold you will also have to get the same info from your customers

When engaging in the gold trade, it is essential to comply with Know Your Customer (KYC) and Anti-Money Laundering (AML) regulations. As a gold dealer, you are required to verify the identity of your clients through the KYC process. This involves collecting and validating personal information, such as government-issued identification, proof of address, and other relevant documents.

Regular sellers, such as you will become, must complete a KYC/AML form to ensure transparency and traceability of transactions. Additionally, both buyers and sellers must adhere to AML regulations to prevent the laundering of illicit funds. This includes monitoring transactions for suspicious activities, maintaining accurate records, and reporting any unusual or suspicious transactions to the relevant authorities. By following these regulations, gold dealers can operate within the legal framework and contribute to the integrity of the financial system.

When you have settled on around three gold buyers and you have approached each in turn, you need to gain understanding of the following.

1/ Their buying - in prices

If you ask most gold buyers what they pay they will tell you a figure and then say that is 98% of spot , for example. It is essential to understand what spot price actually is.

Kitco and Goldprice.org are both online sites that give you the spot price for precious metals. The LBMA spot price is something you need to know daily and further exploration of this is required.

The London Bullion Market Association (LBMA) spot price is the benchmark price for gold and silver traded on the global over-the-counter (OTC) market. It is widely recognized and used by traders, investors, and institutions as the standard for pricing precious metals. Here's a detailed description:

Key Features of the LBMA Spot Price

i. Establishment and Authority:

- The LBMA is a globally respected organization that sets standards for the bullion market.

- The spot price is established by the LBMA and is considered the most accurate and reliable indicator of the current value of gold and silver.

ii. Price Determination:

- The LBMA spot price is derived from electronic trading on the OTC market, which operates 24 hours a day.

- It reflects the most recent transaction prices, ensuring that it is a real-time representation of market conditions.

iii. Price Fixing Process:

- Twice daily (at 10:30 AM and 3:00 PM London time), the LBMA conducts a price fixing session for gold known as the LBMA Gold Price.

- This process involves a group of participating banks and financial institutions that collectively agree on a price that balances buy and sell orders.

iv. **Global Influence:**

- The LBMA spot price serves as a reference for the pricing of gold and silver products worldwide.
- It influences the pricing of futures contracts, ETFs, and other financial instruments linked to precious metals.

v. **Transparency and Trust:**

- The LBMA maintains high standards of transparency and integrity in its price setting processes.
- It regularly audits and accredits its members to ensure compliance with rigorous market practices.

vi6. **Utility for Stakeholders:**

- **Traders and Investors:** Use the LBMA spot price to make informed trading and investment decisions.
- **Jewellery and Manufacturing:** Industries rely on the spot price to price their products and manage supply chains.
- **Central Banks and Governments:** Use it as a reference for reserves management and economic policies.

vii. **Accessibility:**

- The LBMA spot price is published and accessible through various financial news platforms, the LBMA website, and market data providers.

Conclusion

The LBMA spot price is a crucial element of the global precious metals market, providing a reliable and transparent benchmark for the valuation of gold and silver. Its influence extends across multiple sectors, ensuring that market participants have a consistent and trustworthy reference point for their transactions.

So, you need to know what percentage of the LBMA spot price your buyer will offer you. Aim for 97% plus for gold and 93% plus for silver platinum palladium etc . No one truly pays 100% of the spot price for scrap gold.

Important maths calculating percentage of Spot price.

Gold buyers often state "I'm paying 98% of spot or today's rate is 97% of the LBMA spot price. To be able to properly compare these buyers you have to know what percentage of spot they pay.

To convert the LBMA daily troy ounce price to £ per gram just follow this formula (remembering a troy ounce is 31.1 grams whilst a cooking ounce is 28 grams and irrelevant here)

LBMA price x percentage of spot paid by buyer divided by 31.1 divided by 24 x the actual carat.

So, let's say the gold price is shown by Kitco as £1860. This means that an ounce of PURE/24k gold is £1860, now divide by 31.1 to get the pure price per ounce (1 troy ounce equals 31.1grams) This equals £59.80 per gram of pure gold. Now if we are working out the price for 9 carat, we would then divide £59.80 by 24 then multiply by 9 which equals £22.42 per gram for 9 carat. For 18 it would be £59.80 /24 x18 = £44.84 Simples?

Not quite this still gives the price at 100% of the LBMA price, but if your buyer pays 98% of spot then you would have to multiply the result by 0.98 (to get 98% of the price i.e. £22.42 x0.98 = £21.97 for 9 and £43.94 for 18 carat gold. If that is what your buyer pays you will obviously set your percentage lower to be able to buy from the Public and sell on.

Silver is slightly different to calculate. The LBMA ounce price today for pure silver is silver is £21.90 per troy ounce. What is this per gram of sterling silver?

First divide the spot price i.e. £21.90 by 31.1 to get price of pure silver per gram i.e. in this case 21.90/31.1 = 0.704p per gram. Then divide the pure silver figure by 999(pure silver purity) and multiply by 925 (i.e. sterling silver purity 925/1000) i.e. 0.704/999 x925 = 0.651p per gram, but again that is for 100% of the LBMA spot Most silver buyers will pay you 93% of the LBMA spot silver price i.e. 0.651 x 93% = 0.6054

Practice this maths until it becomes second nature. It is the math that all gold buyers use though the percentages they will offer you will be more than the percentage you will offer the Public.

2/ The best times of the day/week to sell to them

Fit in with your gold buyer. Ask them the best time for you to visit them. It is just common-sense courtesy, but from your point of view timing the sale correctly is an invaluable aid to your cashflow.

3/ What they will and won't buy.

If they only want scrap then you will need to find buyers also of non-scrap items e.g. a diamond merchant or a seller of antique, pristine rings, because you will come across these items.

4/ How they pay and how quickly (essential for cashflow)

This vital information will help you to plan your cashflow better. Avoid gold buyers that take too long to pay out and anything more than 24 hours really will just sap your cashflow, making you wait around until funds are released. Get your timing right.

5/ Whether or not they use XRF analysis

As we have discussed xrf is the latest fastest and most accurate testing. If your gold buyer does not use XRF he will not be able to distinguish between 21, 22 and 23 carat gold for example, nor tell the difference between 23 and 24 carat. Acid is just not that precise. This is not acceptable nor workable for you. Insist on XRF testing and only use gold buyers with this facility.

Besides, having a friendly go-to place for xrf analysis can be worth its weight in gold to you.

Imagine you just bought 5 9 carat gold rings from a customer, yet he has an 18-carat bracelet that is not hallmarked. With trust you could take that item down to your friendly buyer and use his xrf testing machine to confirm the result, following which you can either buy or reject the item. Never forget to offer a small payment for such a service. XRF machines cost upwards of £20,000 with a costly maintenance schedule, so every time it is used it incurs a cost.

In fact, there are many ways a friendly gold buying organization can be of further help to you.

i/ As we just mentioned XRF analysis.

ii/ help with cashflow.

A gold buyer I sold to for 5 years was advancing me regular weekly sums of £40,000 to help my cashflow. This is NOT altruism; they gained a loyal customer.

iii/ Tips and Advice

In the early days I learned a tremendous amount by just asking my gold dealer e.g. 9ct ft+bk means gold plated not real 9cart gold; that many bangles have a non-gold i.e. metal wire running through them and some are filled with resin etc.; that Asian gold must be scraped before XRF testing because the 21/22ct gold can be dipped in 24carat , giving misleading reasons…and so on.

Now that you have established a team of three friendly gold buyers all waiting for you to sell gold to them you are ready to start buying gold and silver.

Summary: Chapter 4. Securing Your Buyer

In this chapter, the importance of securing a reliable buyer for your gold and silver transactions is emphasized. Understanding the traits of good gold buyers, practicing due diligence, and building strong relationships with reputable buyers are crucial steps before starting to purchase gold and silver. These points are all summarised below.

Key Traits of Good Gold Buyers:

1. **Customer First:**
   - Good gold buyers prioritize customer needs and provide excellent service. Avoid those who are rude or unhelpful.

2. **Honesty:**
   - Honest gold buyers weigh items properly using calibrated scales and make the weights visible to sellers. They also advertise prices transparently and don't obscure the true payout rate.

3. **Meticulousness:**
   - Good gold buyers carefully check each piece of jewellery. They take the time to evaluate items accurately without rushing through the process.

4. **Integrity:**
   - They honour their advertised prices and don't use tricks to reduce the payout. Watch out for practices like deducting

too much weight for non-metal parts.

5. **Caution with Purity:**
   ◦ Reliable buyers don't gamble on the purity of gold. If unsure, they leave the item out instead of making uncertain offers. This cautious approach should be mirrored by sellers.

6. **Knowledge of Metals and Math:**
   ◦ Competent gold buyers are well-versed in identifying carats and performing accurate calculations. Avoid those who are unsure or make frequent mistakes.

7. **Fairness:**
   ◦ Good gold buyers are not greedy. They pay fair prices and don't constantly try to pinch a few extra pounds through dubious excuses.

Securing Reliable Buyers:

- **Google Search:**

  ◦ Use search terms like "sell gold" or "gold buyers UK" to find potential buyers. Look for companies that publish their buying prices and check their reviews.

- **Phone and Physical Visits:**

  ◦ Contact potential buyers and build a rapport. Ensure they are willing to take on new trade customers and comply with KYC and AML regulations.

- **Evaluating Buyers:**

- Confirm their buying prices relative to the LBMA spot price, best times for selling, items they buy, payment methods and timing, and whether they use XRF analysis.

- **Math for Pricing:**

  - Understand how to convert the LBMA daily troy ounce price to price per gram. Practice these calculations to become proficient.

Takeaway Points:

1. **Prioritize Customer Service:** Good gold buyers put customers first, providing honest and meticulous service.

2. **Seek Transparency:** Ensure buyers clearly advertise their prices and don't obscure the true payout rate.

3. **Build Relationships:** Establish strong connections with reliable buyers to facilitate smooth transactions and cash flow.

4. **Verify Methods:** Use buyers who employ accurate testing methods, such as XRF analysis, to ensure precise evaluations.

5. **Understand Pricing:** Master the math for converting the LBMA spot price to price per gram to negotiate effectively.

By following these guidelines and securing reliable buyers, you can confidently start buying gold and silver, ensuring fair transactions and building a successful business.

CHAPTER 5. STARTING YOUR ON-LINE GOLD BUSINESS

Step 1/ Cost Your Business & Establish your Buying Selling margins Is this feasible?

You know what the companies you are going to sell to, will pay you. The question quickly becomes what will you be paying The Public? Rates vary wildly in the UK and abroad, with some well-known postal gold TV companies paying less than 75% of the LBMA, whilst others offer the Public up to 95-6%.

As a rule of thumb aim to sit around 4-5% behind your gold buyers. So, if they offer you 97% aim to pay the Public around 92%. For every £1000 of gold, you buy you would be making around £50 profit, for just buying and selling. Of course, many secondary gold buyers pay a lot less than this some less than 50% even, but there is an old adage in the gold industry, "pay more get more" 10% percent less i.e. around 88% is still an effective margin. You may buy in less but will make more profit per customer i.e. £100 for every £1000 spent.

The assumption I am making is that you pretty much know how to run a small business. You will have fixed costs e.g. rent rates staff etc that have to be covered every month. If you assume that your fixed costs are 1000 per month and you are buying gold at 90% of the spot price at £22 per gram and selling it to you buyer at 97% of spot i.e. at £23.71 and assuming it's all 9 carat gold for simplicity .

To cover your £1000 of office fixed costs, you will need to buy and sell approximately 584 grams of gold. And at your price of £22 per gram you would need to buy £12848 of gold in a month to make £1000 and cover your costs.

In reality you could visit your gold buyer 5 times a week or more and sell small amounts of gold, so you do not actually need £12848 of working capital. When I first started out with £50. I spent £50 on gold and returned several times per day to the buyer to sell more and yes, the money grew rapidly. Of course, as I have stated again and again in this book you will need a friendly gold buyer, one who is happy to see you, one who is helpful and who pays out fast. The buyers that trust you and who value your business may be able to help you with cashflow by advancing funds, but this takes many months of trust . The key point here is that you do not need a huge bank balance to start in this business.

Full-Time or part Time

Either works. You can do this business part-time, armed with all the information in this book, or you could do it full time.

Post Or In person.

Do both. See customers in person, but also accept postal gold from customers.

Step 2 Think of a Name For Your Business

Pick a name that will help any website you come up with , rise in e.g. Google search listings. This is a competitive field, and a good name will help no end. If you include in your name the name of a geographical area, consider that in that area your listing may well become prominent, but what about the rest of the country? Always include the word gold in your name and what you are about if possible Good names include the following.

Gold Buyers UK,

  Britannia Gold Traders

Gold Secure Buyers

  Regal Gold Traders

PureGold Buyers

  Sovereign Gold Traders

Gold Harvest Buyers

  Prestige Gold Buyers

  Golden Sovereign Traders

UK Gold Buyers

Golden Exchange UK

Britannia Gold Traders

  Gold Secure UK

  Regal Gold Buyers

  PureGold Collectors

Sovereign Gold Deals

  Gold Harvest UK

Prestige Gold Trade

Golden Sovereign Exchange

UK Gold Hub

Of course, some of these names may well be in use so do check first.

Consider also making your business more location specific. If you live in Coventry for example, names such as Coventry Gold Buyers, Coventry Gold and Silver or even Sell Gold Coventry could be good names. Of course, your catchment area will be a lot smaller, but in this day and aged people tend to travel less with their valuables. Your choice!

Step 3: Decide what to Buy where to buy from and how.

What to Buy

As discussed, you will be looking to purchase scrap gold, which includes unwanted, unfashionable, worn, or damaged gold jewellery, as well as gold coins and bars, such as Sovereigns and half Sovereigns. Scrap gold refers to any gold items that are no longer in their prime condition or are considered out of style and thus are typically melted down and repurposed. This category also encompasses silver coins, bars, and jewellery that are no longer wanted or are damaged.

In addition to scrap metals, you may also consider buying diamond rings and vintage or antique items, such as pendants. These items fall under the category of fine jewellery, which is characterized by its high craftsmanship, often involving precious stones and intricate designs. Fine jewellery is typically valued higher than scrap gold due to its artistic and material value. For these types of purchases, you might need to pay a premium price.

To assist with this, I have included a brief chapter at the end of this book specifically dedicated to fine jewellery and other non-scrap items. This chapter provides guidance on the different approach required for selling fine jewellery, which often involves locating specialized buyers and employing different sales strategies compared to dealing with scrap gold and silver. All other chapters in this book will focus on the aspects related to scrap gold, silver, and similar materials.

How and Where to Buy

1. Small Office and/or Out & About

When I started out, I made appointments to visit members of the public at their homes. This works well, but in this day and age, it could be a massive security risk. So never visit rough areas, always use Google Maps to confirm a destination, and never carry cash—pay via bank transfer instead. I also ran around boot sales and antique auctions but soon rented serviced offices in Manchester and never looked back.

If you do decide on a small office so that members of the public can visit you to sell their gold to you, make sure it is safe and secure. Business centres are one way to go or serviced offices. Either way, a premises establishes you in the marketplace.

2/ Postal and In person

Whether in person or via post, the buying process is the same. With premises not only can you see customers face to face, more importantly you can also receive gold via post (which you could also do via a PO Box number . Obviously, the postal service would take longer to establish, but it still is a great source of income for you.

But sitting in an office making appointments for customers to come to see you, and receiving post, or you going to see them, are not the only ways to buy gold.

Here are several other places to buy scrap gold from the public:

NB make sure you have business cards printed and hand then out like confetti. Someone is going to need you.

3. Boot Sales (Car Boot Sales)

- Community events where individuals sell personal items from the back of their cars.

- Ideal for finding gold jewellery, coins, and other valuable items at potentially lower prices.

- Arrive early to get the best deals and bring your testing equipment to verify the authenticity of items.

4. Gold Parties

- Organize or attend gold parties where people bring their gold items to sell. These events can be social and profitable.

- Offer to appraise and buy gold items on the spot.

5. Friends and Family

- Let friends and family know that you buy gold. They might have items they want to sell or know someone who does.

- This network can provide a steady stream of potential deals and can be encouraged with referral promotions like e.g. "refer-a-friend & receive a silver coin".

6. Auctions

- **Antique Auctions**: Look for local auction houses that specialize in antiques and collectibles.

- **Online Auctions**: Websites like eBay can be a valuable source for gold items. Ensure you buy from reputable sellers and verify item authenticity.

- **Estate Auctions**: Estate sales and auctions are excellent sources of gold. They often feature high-quality items being liquidated from estates.

7. Antique Markets

- Antique markets and fairs are venues where dealers sell vintage and antique items, including gold jewellery and coins.

- These markets can be a goldmine for finding unique and valuable pieces.

- Build relationships with regular dealers to get better deals and early access to new items.

8. Flea Markets

- Flea markets offer a wide variety of goods from individual sellers.

- Great places to find gold items at bargain prices.

- Always test items for authenticity before purchasing.

9. Pawn Shops

- Pawn shops frequently deal in gold items, including jewellery, coins, and bullion.

- They may offer good deals, especially if they need to move inventory quickly.

- Establish relationships with local pawn shop owners to get notified of new gold items.

10. Jewellery Stores

- Some jewellery stores buy and sell second-hand gold items.

- They might offer discounts on items that have been in stock for a while.

- Visiting these stores regularly can lead to good finds.

11. Online Marketplaces

- Websites like Craigslist, Facebook Marketplace, and Gumtree are platforms where individuals sell gold items.
- Be cautious and meet sellers in safe, public places.

- **Always test items before finalizing the purchase.**

12 Local Community Groups and Forums

- Join local community groups and online forums where people buy and sell items.

- Look for posts about gold items for sale and connect with the sellers.

- These groups can be a great way to find deals and build a network of contacts.

13. Estate Sales

- Estate sales are often held to liquidate the belongings of a deceased person. These sales can offer high-quality gold items.

- Attend these sales regularly and build relationships with estate sale organizers.

14 Advertisements

- Place ads in local newspapers, online classifieds, and community bulletin boards indicating that you buy gold.

- Create business cards and flyers to distribute in your community.

- This proactive approach can bring sellers directly to you.

Safety Tips for Buying Scrap Gold

1. **Always Verify Authenticity**: Use your testing tools to confirm the gold's purity before purchasing.

2. **Stay Safe**: When meeting sellers, choose public places and avoid carrying large amounts of cash.

3. **Build Relationships**: Establish connections with regular sellers and dealers to get better deals and early access to items.

4. **Be Professional**: Maintain a professional demeanour and provide receipts for all transactions to build trust and credibility.

proper precautions, you can successfully grow your gold-buying business.

Step 4 Construct a website

These days almost everything is online and as a gold buyer you will benefit greatly from having your own website . This website will detail what you do/buy and how, when and where menu headings should be.

1. Home

2. About Us

3. Services
   - Gold Buying
   - Silver Buying
   - Platinum & Palladium
   - Rolled Gold Buying

4. What We Buy
   - Gold Jewellery
   - Gold Coins
   - Gold Bars
   - Scrap Gold
   - Bullion
   - Silver
   - Platinum/Palladium
   - Rolled Gold

5. Sell Your Gold
   - How It Works
   - Get a Quote
   - Shipping Instructions
   - In-Person Appointments

6. Prices
    ◦ Current Gold Prices
    ◦ Historical Prices

7. FAQs

8. Blog

9. Contact Us
    ◦ Location & Hours
    ◦ Contact Form
    ◦ Customer Support

10. Legal & Compliance
    ◦ KYC/AML Information
    ◦ Privacy Policy
    ◦ Terms and Conditions

These headings should help visitors navigate your site easily and find the information they need. Not all pages will be needed in the first instance, but the website will grow as time.

Make sure that you get your site listed with Google passes and various information is required by customers.

Getting your site listed on Google and optimizing its visibility involves several key steps. Here's a brief guide to help you:

1. Google Search Console

a. Set Up Google Search Console:

- Go to the Google Search Console website.
- Click on "Start now" and sign in with your Google account.
- Add your website by entering its URL and choosing the appropriate property type (domain or URL prefix).

- Verify ownership of your website by following the provided verification methods (e.g., HTML file upload, DNS record, Google Analytics).

b. Submit Your Sitemap:

- Once verified, go to the "Sitemaps" section in the left-hand menu.

- Enter the URL of your sitemap (e.g., www.birminghamgoldcompany.co.uk/sitemap.xml).

- Click "Submit" to help Google crawl and index your site more efficiently.

2. Google My Business

a. Create or Claim Your Business Listing:

- Go to the Google My Business website.

- Click on "Manage now" and sign in with your Google account.

- Enter your business name and address. If your business is already listed, claim it; otherwise, create a new listing.

b. Verify Your Business:

- Follow the verification process, which usually involves receiving a postcard with a verification code at your business address.

- Enter the code in your Google My Business account to complete the verification.

c. Optimize Your Listing:

- Add accurate and complete information about your business, including address, phone number, website, hours of operation, and business categories.

- Upload high-quality photos of your business.

- Encourage customers to leave reviews and respond to them promptly.

3. Basic SEO Practices

a. Keyword Research:

- Identify relevant keywords for your business using tools like Google Keyword Planner, SEMrush, or Ahrefs.
- Focus on keywords related to gold buying, gold prices, and your location. e.g. sell gold, gold buyers best prices for gold, cash for gold etc.

b. On-Page SEO:

- Optimize your website's meta titles, meta descriptions, headers (H1, H2), and content with relevant keywords.
- Ensure your website is mobile-friendly, has fast loading times, and provides a good user experience.

c. Content Creation:

- Regularly update your website with high-quality content, such as blog posts about gold buying tips, market trends, and FAQs.

d. Backlinks:

- Build backlinks by getting other reputable websites to link to your content. This can be achieved through guest blogging, partnerships, and creating valuable resources.

4. Analytics and Monitoring

a. Google Analytics:

- Set up Google Analytics to track your website's traffic and user behaviour. This data can help you make informed decisions about your SEO strategy.

b. Monitor Performance:

- Regularly check Google Search Console for performance reports, crawl errors, and search queries that drive traffic to your site.

- Use insights from Google Analytics and Search Console to continuously optimize your website.

By following these steps, you can effectively list your site on Google, enhance its visibility, and attract more visitors to your gold buying business.

Step 5 Use Social Media

Getting your gold buying business onto social media effectively involves creating engaging profiles, posting valuable content, and interacting with your audience. Here's a brief guide:

1. Choosing the Right Platforms

a. Facebook:

- Create a business page.
- Share updates, market news, promotions, and customer testimonials.
- Use Facebook Ads to target potential customers in your area.

b. Instagram:

- Set up a business profile.
- Post high-quality images of gold items, behind-the-scenes content, and infographics about gold buying.
- Utilize stories, reels, and IGTV to share more engaging content.

c. Twitter:

- Create a business account.
- Share quick updates, market insights, and engage in industry-related conversations.
- Use hashtags relevant to your business, like #GoldBuying, #GoldPrices, #InvestInGold.

d. LinkedIn:

- Create a company page.
- Share professional insights, industry news, and connect with other businesses.

- Publish articles and posts that establish your authority in the gold buying industry.

e. YouTube:

- Set up a channel.

- Upload videos about the gold buying process, market trends, customer testimonials, and educational content about gold.

- Optimize video titles, descriptions, and tags with relevant keywords.

2. Profile Optimization

a. Complete Your Profile:

- Ensure all business information is accurate and consistent across platforms.

- Use a professional logo and cover photo.

- Write a compelling bio or description that includes relevant keywords.

b. Link to Your Website:

- Include your website URL in the bio or about section of each social media profile.

- Use call-to-action buttons (e.g., "Contact Us," "Learn More") where available.

3. Content Strategy

a. Content Calendar:

- Plan and schedule posts in advance to maintain a consistent posting schedule.

- Mix different types of content: educational posts, promotional offers, customer stories, market updates, and behind-the-scenes.

b. Engaging Content:

- Share high-quality images and videos of gold products.

- Post informative content about gold market trends, investment tips, and FAQs.

- Create interactive content like polls, quizzes, and Q&A sessions.

c. Hashtags and Keywords:

- Use relevant hashtags to increase visibility.

- Incorporate keywords in your posts to improve searchability.

4. Engagement and Community Building

a. Interact with Followers:

- Respond promptly to comments, messages, and reviews.

- Engage with your audience by asking questions and encouraging discussions.

b. Collaborate with Influencers:

- Partner with local influencers or industry experts to reach a wider audience.

- Consider running giveaways or promotions with them to attract more followers.

c. Monitor and Adjust:

- Use analytics tools provided by each platform to track the performance of your posts.

- Adjust your strategy based on what content resonates most with your audience.

5. Advertising

a. Targeted Ads:

- Use the advertising features on each platform to create targeted ads.

- Define your audience based on demographics, interests, and behaviours.

b. Promotions:

- Run promotions and special offers to attract new customers.

- Use paid promotions to boost important posts and increase reach.

By following these steps, you can effectively establish a strong social media presence for your gold buying business, engage with your audience, and drive more traffic to your website.

Step 6 Offline promotion.

Websites, even with huge social media efforts need a little offline push quite often. As a newly minted gold buyer your efforts should be both local and national

Local

Approach key businesses in your area that might get gold in, e.g. charity shops, auctions, antique and collectibles dealers . Leave them your business card , you never know ! Attend local boot sales and fairs where you can leave flyers and promo material and most importantly your business card.

National

consider advertising via AdWords or in physical newspapers and lifestyle magazines, this is something for when you have established your business.

But an ad, whether local or national followed by a door-knocking campaign, whilst some may declare old-hat, still works well in this day and age, give away your business cards.

Step7 Secure your Buyers.

You have already spoken to and visited the gold buyers you wish to use for scrap, by this stage, so write to them all confirming that you will be selling gold to them and giving all your details so as to comply with KYC and AML regulations. Now is also the time to approach some buyers of non-scrap items. The Public you are going to serve will have both scrap and non-scrap items, as discussed above. Non-scrap may well be less common and even then, only a few items might be marketable, so before you even consider buying nonscrap items e.g. a diamond ring, a set of pearls etc it is best to phone around and get some contacts. Confirm with these buyers that you can send an image and they will get back to you asap!

Step 8 Open a Business bank Account.

You are clearly going to need a bank account so that you can pay your customers payments will often be made using the faster payments system so a bank like Tide or Monzo or a regular High St. bank with online banking facilities will suffice.

Chapter 5 Summary: Starting Your Online Gold Business

Chapter 5 provides a detailed roadmap for launching an online gold buying business. The chapter outlines crucial steps for establishing and running the business, focusing on cost management, branding, sourcing gold, building a website, utilizing social media, offline promotion, and securing buyers. The goal is to create a sustainable business model that balances competitive buying prices with profitable selling margins.

Key Points:

1. **Cost Your Business & Establish Buying Selling Margins:**
   - Determine the feasibility of your business by calculating buying and selling margins.
   - Aim to pay the public around 4-5% less than what your gold buyers offer you.
   - Consider fixed costs like rent, rates, and staff, and calculate the amount of gold needed to cover these costs.
   - Develop a relationship with a trustworthy gold buyer for better cash flow management.

2. **Full-Time or Part-Time Operation:**
   - The business can be run either full-time or part-time, depending on your availability and goals.
   - Utilize both in-person and postal methods to maximize reach and flexibility.

3. **Think of a Name for Your Business:**

- Choose a name that helps with search engine visibility and includes keywords like "gold" and potentially a geographic area.
- Examples of good names include Gold Buyers UK, Britannia Gold Traders, and Prestige Gold Buyers.
- Ensure the chosen name is unique and check its availability.

4. **Decide What to Buy, Where to Buy From, and How**:
   - Focus on scrap gold, including unwanted, unfashionable, worn, or damaged jewellery, as well as gold coins and bars.
   - Consider buying fine jewellery, diamond rings, and vintage items, but be prepared to pay a premium.
   - Sources for buying include small offices, boot sales, gold parties, friends and family, auctions, antique markets, flea markets, pawn shops, jewellery stores, online marketplaces, local community groups, estate sales, and advertisements.
   - Ensure authenticity and stay safe by meeting sellers in public places and avoiding carrying large amounts of cash.

5. **Construct a Website**:
   - Create a user-friendly website with clear sections: Home, About Us, Services, What We Buy, Sell Your Gold, Prices, FAQs, Blog, Contact Us, and Legal & Compliance.

- Optimize the site for search engines by setting up Google Search Console and Google My Business.
- Implement SEO practices, including keyword research, on-page optimization, and content creation.

6. **Use Social Media**:
   - Establish a presence on platforms like Facebook, Instagram, Twitter, LinkedIn, and YouTube.
   - Optimize profiles, create engaging content, and interact with your audience.
   - Use targeted ads and promotions to reach potential customers.

7. **Offline Promotion**:
   - Engage in local promotions by networking with businesses, attending boot sales and fairs, and distributing business cards and flyers.
   - Consider national advertising through Google Ads and print media once the business is established.
   - Door-knocking campaigns can be effective for local outreach.

8. **Secure Your Buyers**:
   - Confirm relationships with gold buyers for scrap transactions, ensuring compliance with KYC and AML regulations.
   - Establish contacts with buyers for non-scrap items and confirm their interest

and criteria for purchasing.

9. Open a Business bank Account.

Take-Away Points:

- **Cost Management**: Accurately calculate buying and selling margins to ensure profitability.
- **Versatile Operations**: Adapt your business model to suit full-time or part-time availability and utilize both in-person and postal methods.
- **Effective Branding**: Choose a business name that enhances visibility and clearly communicates your services.
- **Diverse Sourcing**: Explore various avenues for purchasing scrap gold and fine jewellery to maximize opportunities.
- **Online Presence**: Build and optimize a user-friendly website and maintain an active, engaging presence on social media.
- **Local and National Promotion**: Combine online and offline promotional strategies to reach a broader audience.
- **Network Building**: Develop strong relationships with gold buyers and other key contacts to ensure smooth operations and reliable sales channels.

By following these steps and leveraging both online and offline strategies, you can establish a successful online gold buying business with a solid foundation and growth potential.

CHAPTER 6
UNDERSTANDING REGULATIONS FOR BUYING GOLD & SILVER IN THE UK

NB These regulations etc relate to the UK. Check the various regulations in your country to ensure that your business is feasible.

As a scrap gold buyer, it's crucial to understand and comply with various regulations governing the purchase of gold and silver in the UK. These regulations are in place to ensure fair trade practices, prevent money laundering, and protect both buyers and sellers. This chapter will cover the essential regulations, including Know Your Customer (KYC), Anti-Money Laundering (AML), the High Value Dealer (HVD) scheme, and compliance with trading standards for weights and measures.

Remember when you first start out, some of this won't apply and there is no point losing sight of the growth potential of your business by getting tied up with red tape. However, the law is the law, and a thorough working knowledge is required.

Know Your Customer (KYC)

KYC regulations require businesses to verify the identity of their customers. This is a critical step in preventing fraud and money laundering. Here's what you need to do:

1. **Customer Identification**:
   - Verify the customer's identity using official documents such as a passport, driving license, or national ID card.
   - Collect and record the customer's personal details, including their full name, address, and date of birth.

2. **Transaction Monitoring**:
   - Keep detailed records of all transactions, including the amount of gold or silver purchased, the date of the transaction, and the customer's details.
   - Monitor transactions for unusual or suspicious activity that might indicate money laundering.

Anti-Money Laundering (AML)

AML regulations are designed to prevent the use of the financial system for money laundering and terrorist financing. As a gold buyer, you must implement AML practices:

1. **Risk Assessment**:
   - Conduct a risk assessment to identify and understand the money laundering risks associated with your business.
   - Implement policies and procedures to mitigate these risks.

2. **Customer Due Diligence (CDD)**:
   - Perform CDD by verifying the identity of your customers and understanding the nature and purpose of their transactions.
   - Enhanced Due Diligence (EDD) should be applied for higher-risk customers and transactions.

3. **Record Keeping**:
   - Maintain records of all transactions, customer identification documents, and risk assessments for at least five years.
   - Ensure that records are easily accessible for inspection by regulatory authorities.

4. **Reporting Suspicious Activity**:
   - Report any suspicious transactions or activities to the National Crime Agency (NCA) using a Suspicious Activity Report (SAR).

High Value Dealer (HVD) Scheme

If you handle cash transactions of €10,000 or more (or the equivalent in any currency), you are considered a High Value Dealer and must comply with specific regulations: My advice though would be to never give more than e.g. a couple of thousand and avoid this complication. Having too much cash is a dangerous security concern in this day and age and electronic transfers are just so much safer, as is a cheque!

1. **Registration**:
   ◦ Register with HM Revenue and Customs (HMRC) as a High Value Dealer.

2. **Customer Identification**:
   ◦ Verify the identity of customers involved in high-value cash transactions.

3. **Compliance with AML**:
   ◦ Implement AML policies and procedures as discussed above.

Weights and Measures

Accurate measurement is vital in the gold and silver trade. Compliance with weights and measures regulations ensures fair transactions and builds trust with your customers:

1. **Calibrated Scales**:
    - Use scales that are calibrated and certified by trading standards to ensure accuracy.
    - Regularly check and maintain your scales to avoid discrepancies.

2. **Recording Weights**:
    - Always weigh gold and silver items in the presence of the customer and record the weight accurately.
    - Ensure that your scales display weights in grams, as this is the standard measurement for precious metals.

3. **Price Transparency**:
    - Clearly display and explain the current market prices of gold and silver to your customers.
    - Ensure that customers understand how the price is calculated based on the weight and purity of the metal.

Trading Standards

Trading standards regulations ensure that businesses operate fairly and transparently. As a gold buyer, you must adhere to these standards:

1. **Honest Advertising**:
   - Ensure that all advertising and marketing materials are truthful and not misleading.
   - Accurately represent the value and purity of the gold and silver you are buying.

2. **Fair Trading Practices**:
   - Treat all customers fairly and with respect.
   - Provide clear and accurate information about the buying process and the factors that affect the value of their items.

3. **Handling Complaints**:
   - Have a clear process for handling customer complaints and disputes.
   - Address complaints promptly and fairly to maintain trust and credibility.

Conclusion

Understanding and complying with these regulations is essential for running a successful and lawful gold buying business in the UK. By implementing KYC, AML, HVD, weights and measures, and trading standards practices, you can ensure that your business operates ethically and transparently. This not only protects you and your customers but also enhances your reputation in the marketplace.

In the next chapter, we will delve deeper into the practical aspects of evaluating and purchasing fine jewellery and non-scrap items, which often require a different approach and understanding.

CHAPTER 7. COMMON FAKED GOLD AND SILVER ITEMS

As a novice gold buyer entering the UK market, it's crucial to be aware of the various counterfeit gold and silver items you might encounter. The lucrative nature of precious metals has attracted a plethora of counterfeiters who produce fake items that can easily deceive inexperienced buyers. This chapter aims to equip you with the knowledge needed to identify and avoid these common fakes, ensuring that your investments are both genuine and valuable.

In the following sections, we'll explore the most frequently encountered counterfeit items, including fake gold sovereigns, tungsten-filled bars, and counterfeit jewellery from renowned brands like Cartier, Nike, and Tiffany & Co. You'll also learn about geographic origin fakes, such as those from Turkey, and the proliferation of counterfeit luxury watches from brands like Rolex and Omega.

Additionally, we'll delve into common fake gold-plated items, counterfeit sterling silver and Mexican silver items, and fake antique coins, including Roman and Greek coins and Morgan dollars. Designer brand fakes, such as Gucci and Louis Vuitton jewellery, as well as fake bars and ingots, are also covered.

Finally, this chapter provides practical tips for identifying fakes, including checking weight and dimensions, inspecting hallmarks, using testing kits, buying from reputable sources, and being cautious of fake certificates. By understanding these common fakes and employing thorough testing methods, you can better protect yourself and make informed decisions in your gold buying endeavours.

1. Fake Sovereigns

- Counterfeit gold sovereign coins are often made with base metals or gold-plated materials.
- They can be difficult to detect without proper testing equipment.

2. Tungsten in Bars

- Tungsten-filled gold bars are a common type of counterfeit due to tungsten's similar density to gold.
- These bars often have a thin layer of gold plating over a tungsten core.

3. Common Fake Jewellery Brands

- **Cartier**
  - Fake Cartier jewellery, including rings, bracelets, and necklaces, are widespread.
  - Often marked with forged hallmarks and serial numbers.
- **Nike**
  - Fake gold-plated or gold-coloured Nike rings and jewellery items.
  - Frequently found with rough stamping and brassy coloration.
- **Tiffany & Co.**
  - Fake Tiffany items, especially silver pieces, are common.
  - Usually, these fakes have inferior

craftsmanship and incorrect hallmarking.

4. **Geographic Origin Fakes**
   ◦ **Turkey**

   - Turkish fakes often include gold jewellery items and coins.
   - They can be sophisticated, sometimes made from lower-purity gold or gold-plated materials.

5. **Luxury Watch Brands**
   ◦ **Rolex**

   - Counterfeit Rolex watches are often made with gold plating or base metals.
   - They may include fake certificates and packaging.

   ◦ **Omega**
   - Fake Omega watches are common, often made with non-precious metals and sold as gold.

6. **Gold-Plated Items**
   ◦ Jewellery items marked as 18k GP (Gold Plated) or similar.
   ◦ Often passed off as solid gold to unwary buyers.

7. **Silver Fakes**
   ◦ **Sterling Silver**

   - Items marked as 925 or Sterling but actually made from base metals or low-purity silver.

   ◦ **Mexican Silver**
   - Fake Mexican silver items often marked as 925 but are silver-plated or base metal.

8. **Fake Antique Coins**
   ◦ **Roman and Greek Coins**

- Commonly reproduced using modern techniques and materials.
  - **Morgan Dollars**
    - Silver-plated replicas often passed off as genuine.

9. **Designer Brand Fakes**
   - **Gucci**
     - Fake Gucci jewellery, including gold and silver-plated items.
     - Often lacks the craftsmanship and hallmarks of genuine pieces.
   - **Louis Vuitton**
     - Counterfeit Louis Vuitton items, especially bracelets and rings, are frequently seen.

10. **Fake Bars and Ingots**
    - **1 oz Gold Bars**
      - Frequently counterfeited using base metals with a gold-plated exterior.
    - **Silver Ingots**
      - Fake silver bars made from base metals, sometimes with silver plating.

Tips for Identifying Fakes:

- **Check Weight and Dimensions**: Authentic items should match official specifications.
- **Inspect Hallmarks**: Genuine items have precise, well-crafted hallmarks.
- **Use Testing Kits**: Acid tests, XRF analysers, and electronic testers can help verify metal purity.
- **Buy from Reputable Sources**: Purchase from established dealers and avoid suspiciously low prices.
- **Beware of Fake Certificates**: Certificates of authenticity can also be forged.

By being aware of these common fakes and employing thorough testing methods, you can better protect yourself from counterfeit gold and silver items.

CHAPTER 8. BUYING FINE JEWELLERY, VINTAGE, ANTIQUE, DESIGNER,LUXURY ITEMS

We have dealt at length about scrap gold and silver and scrap is your bread and butter so to speak, but what to do with all non-scrap items that will be offered to you is the problem. There is no point letting better items just slip through your fingers and we have already stated that offering scrap prices for such items is not only bad practice and unethical, but it may also well damage your reputation.

Before we discuss how you can build up this side of your business and make no mistake it will take a lot of time and a lot of contacting and discussing items with potential buyers it is important to delve a little deeper into what is and what is not scrap.

As discussed in previous chapters there are several factors that help you to decide what is and what is not scrap.

There are four main factors to take into account when deciding whether a Gold or Silver ring, necklace, bracelet etc is worth more than scrap. The first is what you may be able to sell on i.e.

what items you can buy for over scrap The second is condition, the third is the type of hallmark and the fourth is market demand.

Let's look at each of these factors in turn.

1/ the Type of Item

.While the gold and silver market often revolves around scrap items that are melted down for their raw material value, there are numerous gold and silver items that hold significant value in their original form and sell well second-hand. These items are often small, and their metal weight value is surpassed by their value as an item.

These items are prized for their craftsmanship, brand, historical significance, or unique design. Here's a guide to identifying and understanding these valuable second-hand items.

Gold Items

1. **Fine Jewellery**
   - **Diamond Rings**: Especially those from well-known brands or with high-quality stones.

   - **Vintage and Antique Pendants**: Pieces from eras such as Victorian, Edwardian, or Art Deco.

   - **Gold Bracelets with Gemstones**: Items featuring diamonds, rubies, sapphires, or emeralds.

   - **Gold Necklaces with Precious Stones**: Especially those with intricate designs and high-quality materials.

   - **Gold Earrings with Precious Stones**: Vintage or designer earrings with significant stones.

   - **Designer and Brand-Name Jewellery**: High-end brands like Tiffany & Co., Cartier, and Van Cleef & Arpels.

2. **Gold Coins**
   - **Rare or Collectible Gold Coins**: Coins with historical significance or limited editions.

   - **Historical Gold Coins**: Coins from ancient civilizations or important historical periods.

   - **Limited Edition Gold Coins**: Specially minted coins with unique designs or from notable events.

- **Proof Gold Coins**: High-quality coins with a mirror-like finish, often kept in pristine condition.

3. **Gold Watches**
   - **Luxury Brand Watches**: Brands such as Rolex, Patek Philippe, Omega, and Cartier.

   - **Vintage Gold Watches**: Timepieces from earlier decades, especially those with unique mechanisms.

   - **Gold Pocket Watches**: Antique pocket watches with intricate designs and craftsmanship.

4. **Designer Gold Items**
   - **High-End Designer Jewellery**: Pieces from renowned designers that hold their value due to brand and quality.

   - **Gold Accessories**: Items like belt buckles, cufflinks, and even gold pens from luxury brands.

Silver Items

1. **Fine Silver Jewellery**
     - **Sterling Silver Rings with Gemstones**: Particularly those featuring high-quality stones. .Low grade stone rings are scrap.

     - **Vintage and Antique Silver Pendants**: Pieces from notable historical periods.

     - **Silver Bracelets with Gemstones**: Especially those from recognized designers.

     - **Silver Necklaces with Precious Stones**: Items with intricate craftsmanship and high-quality materials.

     - **Designer and Brand-Name Silver Jewellery**: High-end brands known for their quality and design.

2. **Silver Coins**
     - **Rare or Collectible Silver Coins**: Coins with historical or numismatic value.

     - **Historical Silver Coins**: Coins from ancient times or significant historical events.

     - **Limited Edition Silver Coins**: Coins minted for special occasions or as part of a limited series.

     - **Proof Silver Coins**: Coins with a high-quality finish, often kept in excellent condition.

3. **Silver Watches**
     - **Luxury Brand Silver Watches**: Brands

such as Omega and Cartier.

- **Vintage Silver Watches**: Timepieces from earlier eras with significant craftsmanship.

- **Silver Pocket Watches**: Antique pocket watches valued for their historical and design significance.

4. **Designer Silver Items**
   - **High-End Designer Silver Jewellery**: Pieces from famous designers.

   - **Silver Accessories**: Items like belt buckles, cufflinks, and even pens from luxury brands.

5. **Silverware**
   - **Antique Silver Cutlery**: Sets or individual pieces from notable historical periods.

   - **Silver Tea Sets**: Especially those with intricate designs and from recognized makers Most however are scrap.

   - **Decorative Silver Items**: Vases, trays, and other decorative pieces with artistic value.

Additional Considerations

When dealing with these non-scrap items, it's crucial to:

- **Verify Authenticity**: Ensure items are genuine and not replicas. This may involve checking hallmarks, brand stamps, and getting expert opinions.

- **Assess Condition**: Items in excellent condition with minimal wear and tear fetch higher prices.

- **Understand Market Demand**: Stay updated on market trends to know which items are currently in demand.

- **Build a Network**: Establish connections with collectors, antique dealers, and auction houses to find the best markets for selling these items.

2/ Condition.

As mentioned, identifying such items as listed above is not enough to determine whether they are actually scrap or not . Another important factor is condition.

Condition is everything with regard to Gold /Silver jewellery. Remember that any jeweller will examine a piece of jewellery under a high-powered magnifying glass or loupe. Gold and Silver jewellery may be scratched, chipped, mis-shaped, with a worn shank in the case of a ring or worn links in the case of a necklace or bracelet. The hallmarks can also wear down and be illegible in some cases, making the item very difficult to sell

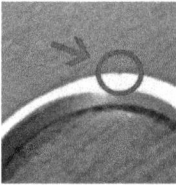

on...

If the ring has stones, then the condition of these stones must also be taken into account. Even diamonds can be scratched or chipped and many softer stones wear badly . Diamonds Rubies and Emeralds are the top-value stones but if they are damaged their value plummets . Diamond retailers make a colossal profit when they sell diamonds, sometimes in excess of 1000% and tiny diamond chips or very small stones have little value in today's marketplace, especially when you consider any jeweller can buy diamonds from a diamond wholesaler at a fraction of

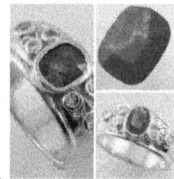

the price a similar diamond might have cost you

The problem is that it costs a lot of money to refurbish a piece of Gold or Silver jewellery and you must take this into account if trying to sell privately. private Buyers will examine every facet of the item and a small scratch can make a sale difficult (Remember also that jewellers etc use a high-powered loupe or magnifying glass so some gemstone wear etc which cannot be seen by the naked eye, will be picked up). At the same time, you also face the usual hassle of finding a private buyer and online selling fees (e.g. eBay) can be very high. Currently auction fees are very high also at around 30% Refurbishing a stone or a

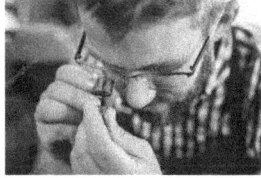

shank can both be costly.

As regards non-jewellery items e.g. antique vestas, or fobs, flatware, objets figurines etc , the same rule applies. If it is damaged and unless the item is extremely rare then it is basically scrap. A dented tea set, a chipped or missing gemstone, a worn hallmark, some solder in a visible place, these are all clues that the item is scrap and should be priced accordingly.

3/ The Type of Hallmark

Many gold and silver jewellery items, such as rings, chains, bracelets, necklaces etc may not be fully hallmarked. They may also have a foreign hallmark. Be aware that any type of hallmark other than a full UK hallmark makes it difficult to sell your item on to a private buyer, because only a full hallmark is proof that the purity of the gold content has been tested by an Assay office. In the UK if a gold item has a foreign hallmark, it would be described in auction as "yellow metal" and not gold, which will impact on its sale price.

4/ Market Demand.

The third factor is of course market demand. fashions and tastes change, and many Gold and Silver jewellery items simply fall out of fashion. At the same time many people shun pre-owned jewellery items as they prefer to buy new. Consider what age group would be interested in purchasing items you consider not to be scrap and remember that certain older age-groups are no longer in the market for jewellery. The key purchase group by age and disposable income is currently the 35-50 age group. Remember also that most stones in 9 carat gold are not valuable. More valuable stones are normally set in 18 carat or Platinum. Of course, there is always a market for certain antique and vintage items of jewellery, especially vintage named items e.g. by Asprey, Tiffany, Cartier etc and these items are certainly not scrap UNLESS they are in rough or damaged condition.

Scrap is easy to spot i.e. broken damaged items, or items out of fashion or with rubbed stones/hallmarks etc and this chapter has helped identify what might not be scrap but for you to value and sell those items identified as non-scrap is more difficult and it will take time for you to learn this part of the business

A quick word about Diamonds Rubies emeralds etc

These are often valued by the Public and whilst becoming a gem dealer is a big and complex enough subject for another book, it would be a wise move for any gold buyer to have at least a brief working knowledge of what to look for. Of course, most of the knowledge you will need will be obtained through your contacts in the trade i.e. your gold buyer and other contacts (see below)

Assessing Diamonds, Rubies, and Emeralds in the UK Market

When starting out in the business of buying and selling scrap gold and gemstones in the UK, accurately assessing the value of diamonds, rubies, and emeralds is crucial for making informed purchasing decisions. Here's a detailed guide to help you get started:

Diamonds

When evaluating diamonds, pay close attention to the 4Cs: Carat, Cut, Colour, and Clarity.

- **Carat**: This refers to the weight of the diamond. Higher carat weights generally mean larger diamonds and therefore, a higher price. For instance, as of the current UK market, the price per carat can vary widely. Approximate prices are:

    - 1/4 carat: £150 to £200
    - 1/2 carat: £300 to £500
    - 3/4 carat: £500 to £900
    - 1 carat: £1,000 to £6,500
    - 2 carats: £2500 to £20,000
    - 3 carats: £3500 to £40,000

- **Cut**: This determines how well the diamond has been shaped and its ability to reflect light, impacting its brilliance. The quality of the cut can significantly affect a diamond's appearance and value.

- **Colour**: Diamonds are graded on a scale from D (colourless) to Z (light yellow or brown). The less colour a diamond has, the more valuable it typically is. Colourless diamonds (D-F) are the most sought after.

- **Clarity**: This measures the presence of internal (inclusions) or external (blemishes) flaws. Clarity grades range from Flawless (no imperfections) to Included (visible flaws). Higher clarity diamonds are more valuable.

Rubies and Emeralds

For rubies and emeralds, the key factors to consider are colour, clarity, and origin.

- **Colour**: The most important factor for both rubies and emeralds. Rubies should have a deep, vibrant red colour, often described as "pigeon's blood." Emeralds are prized for their rich green hue, with a preference for a deep, saturated colour without any yellow or brown tint.

- **Clarity**: Both rubies and emeralds typically have inclusions, but the fewer and less visible they are, the higher the gemstone's value. Eye-clean stones (those with no inclusions visible to the naked eye) are especially valuable.

- **Origin**: The geographical origin of these gemstones can significantly impact their value. For instance, Burmese rubies and Colombian emeralds are considered the finest and thus command higher prices.

Current Market Prices (2024)

The market prices for these gemstones fluctuate, so it's important to stay updated. Here are some general price ranges based on the latest UK market trends:

- **Rubies**:
    - 1 carat: £800 to £12,000
    - 2 carats: £4,000 to £20,000
    - 3 carats: £8,000 to £40,000
- **Emeralds**:
    - 1 carat: £400 to £4,000
    - 2 carats: £1,600 to £12,000
    - 3 carats: £4,000 to £24,000

Further Reading and Resources

To deepen your understanding and stay updated with the latest trends and market prices, consider the following UK-based websites and trade resources:

- **The National Association of Jewellers (NAJ)**: Provides industry news, education, and resources for jewellers in the UK.
- **Gem-A (Gemological Association of Great Britain)**: Offers courses and information on gemology and gemstone grading standards.
- **IGR (International Gemological Reports UK)**: Provides diamond and gemstone grading services. IGR UK
- **Birmingham Assay Office**: Offers independent testing and hallmarking services, along with educational resources.

Understanding these basics and keeping abreast of market trends will help you distinguish between high-quality stones and those that should be treated as scrap, ensuring you make informed purchasing decisions in the UK gemstone market.

Pricing & selling non-scrap items.

There are several approaches to securing prices and sales of non-scrap gold and silver items. It would be best to do all of them as you build up your database of knowledge.

Ask your Gold Buyer

The simplest approach here is just to ask your gold buyer whether he will pay more for these type of non-scrap items. Pin him/her down by asking for specific details of what they would and would not buy . If they say they buy diamonds ask them what size, carat colour and cut for example (see below) . if they say they buy certain Edwardian jewellery again explore what types and how much over scrap or over spot they would give

Antique Dealers/Fairs

Travel to as many fairs and see as many antique dealers as possible hand out your business card and identify what they are keen to buy in, whether diamond rings for example or antique pendants etc. But it is not enough for you to just learn that such and such dealer wants diamond rings. What size of diamond are they looking for? What price range etc? be specific and soon you will have enough contacts to be able to sell fine jewellery to.

Auction Houses & eBay.

Besides scouring auction catalogue sold prices , eBay and other online selling sites provide a wealth of information on the prices these type of items fetch To find actual sold prices on eBay , scroll down the left hand column until you see two boxes i.e. "Sold Items" and "Completed items " Tick both boxes and the green prices you see on the right and actual prices realized.

But eBay and auction sites are also very important to you for another reason. You can use these sites to sell your non-gold items on. You will have paid more than scrap for them, so you are morally free to sell them on at whatever price you feel is right. So, get listing!

Social Media Facebook marketplace
Instagram etc

There are plenty of other places to both get pricing info and to sell your items through. Facebook marketplace is one, also Instagram and even apps like Shpock and Vinted

Conclusions

Spending time talking with dealers and the trade and scouring online auction and sales sites will enable you to learn this difficult marketplace, but remember it is not your main business.

Chapter Summary: Buying Fine Jewellery - Whether Vintage, Antique, or Designer/ Luxury Names

In this chapter, the focus shifts from scrap gold and silver to non-scrap items such as fine jewellery, vintage, antique, and designer pieces. The importance of correctly identifying and valuing these items is emphasized, as offering scrap prices for valuable items can harm your reputation. The chapter outlines several key factors to consider when determining whether a piece is worth more than scrap value, including the type of item, its condition, hallmark, and market demand.

Key Points:

1. **Type of Item**:
   - Certain gold and silver items hold significant value beyond their metal content due to their craftsmanship, brand, historical significance, or unique design.

   - Items to look for include:

     - **Gold Items**: Diamond rings, vintage pendants, gemstone bracelets, designer jewellery (e.g., Tiffany & Co., Cartier), rare and historical gold coins, luxury watches (e.g., Rolex, Patek Philippe), and designer gold accessories.

     - **Silver Items**: Sterling silver jewellery with high-quality gemstones, vintage pendants, designer silver jewellery, rare and historical silver coins, luxury and vintage silver watches, and antique silverware.

2. **Condition**:
    - The condition of jewellery and other items significantly impacts their value. Scratches, chips, worn hallmarks, and damaged stones can reduce the value.
    - Refurbishing costs should be considered when assessing value. High repair costs can turn a potentially valuable item into scrap.

3. **Type of Hallmark**:
    - Full UK hallmarks are essential for selling gold and silver items to private buyers. Foreign hallmarks can lower the item's perceived value and make it harder to sell.

4. **Market Demand**:
    - Market trends and fashion significantly influence the value of jewellery items. Certain age groups and preferences impact what is currently in demand.
    - Antique and vintage items from well-known brands generally retain higher value, provided they are in good condition.

5. **Assessing Diamonds, Rubies, and Emeralds**:
    - **Diamonds**: Evaluate based on the 4Cs (Carat, Cut, Colour, Clarity). Current UK market prices range from £150 to £40,000 depending on size and quality.
    - **Rubies and Emeralds**: Consider colour, clarity, and origin. Prices range from £400 to £40,000 based on carat weight and quality.

6. **Pricing & Selling Non-Scrap Items**:
   - **Gold Buyers**: Ask gold buyers about their interest in non-scrap items and the specifics of what they are looking for.
   - **Antique Dealers/Fairs**: Establish contacts with antique dealers and visit fairs to understand what items they are keen to buy.
   - **Auction Houses & eBay**: Use these platforms to gather pricing information and to sell non-scrap items. Online sites like eBay can provide actual sold prices for similar items.
   - **Social Media**: Utilize Facebook Marketplace, Instagram, Shpock, and Vinted for both pricing research and selling items.

Take-Away Points:

- **Identifying Value**: Not all gold and silver items should be treated as scrap. Understanding the value of vintage, antique, and designer pieces can significantly enhance your business.

- **Condition Matters**: The physical state of jewellery and other items is crucial. Damage and wear can drastically reduce value.

- **Hallmark Significance**: Full UK hallmarks are necessary for maximizing the resale value of gold and silver items.

- **Market Trends**: Stay informed about market demand and trends to effectively price and sell non-scrap items.

- **Networking**: Building a network of buyers, dealers, and collectors is essential for finding the best markets for valuable items.

- **Continuous Learning**: The jewellery market is complex and requires ongoing education and research to navigate successfully.

By focusing on these areas, you can enhance your ability to identify, value, and sell fine jewellery, ensuring that you do not miss out on valuable opportunities and maintain a good reputation in the industry.

A Final Word

I hope that you have enjoyed this book and got from it all the information you need to be a successful gold buyer. All that remains for me to say is keep this book handy, use it as a reference guide where needed and refresh your understanding of it, from time to time as you become an established name in this exciting marketplace.

Remember you do not need huge amounts of capital to be successful in this business, but care, professionalism and due diligence will lead to success....and if you have to return to your gold buyer a few times a day/week to sell what your very limited capital has enabled you to buy...then do it, keep turning over that ever-growing capital!

www.ingramcontent.com/pod-product-compliance
Ingram Content Group UK Ltd.
Pitfield, Milton Keynes, MK11 3LW, UK
UKHW011555300725
7148UKWH00024B/349

9 798335 158817